HUTCHINSON POCKET

The
Sixties

GW00367739

Other titles in the Hutchinson Pocket series:

HUTCHINSON POCKET

The
Sixties

Helicon

Copyright © Helicon Publishing Ltd 1994

All rights reserved

Helicon Publishing Ltd
42 Hythe Bridge Street
Oxford OX1 2EP

Printed and bound in Great Britain by
Unwin Brothers Ltd, Old Woking, Surrey

ISBN 1–85986–020–6

British Cataloguing in Publication Data

A catalogue record for this book is available
from the British Library

Introduction

'Time for a change' – that was the phrase used to describe Britain's political atmosphere when Harold Wilson's Labour administration returned to power in 1964. But the phrase also epitomized the 1960s. This was a decade of hope and dashed hopes: when the power of the media brought to the world stage a charismatic young president of the United States, the first president to be born in this century; when Martin Luther King campaigned for, and promised, a future in which non-whites would have equal rights and status in the most powerful nation on earth. Both men were assassinated before their dreams were fulfilled.

Suddenly, youth culture seemed to be leading the way with new music, new clothes, new arts, and new architecture while those who had provided the stability and economic security for these new freedoms were left bewildered, if not enraged, by what they had spawned. This was the decade when two powers locked horns in the so-called Cold War, and when the world could so easily have seen thermonuclear conflagration over the 'Cuban missile crisis'. Meanwhile, all around the globe smaller nations were shaking off the shackles of their imperial masters in an effort to evolve their own independent futures. In the West young men were growing their hair, young women were shortening their skirts, and Beatlemania brought screaming teenagers to welcome their idols, the 'fab four', at rock concerts and airports. But, on the other side of the world, young GIs and Vietnamese of all ages were at each others' throats and dying in their thousands in a war that brought only losers.

The Sixties distils into one pocket-sized volume the happenings of the most eventful decade since the 1920s. For the 'children of the sixties', to dip into it is to be taken back to the excitement and anticipation of their youth while for their off-spring it is a chance to glean something of the age to which their parents hark back at the drop of a hat. Browse through the book and the significant facet of each event stands out in bold type. Use the index and you can quickly refer to the year of any particular topic. Go to the back of the book and, as well as population, sporting, and other statistics, you will find the titles, artists, and dates of every hit single and album that topped the charts in Britain. With a short introduction to each year, *The Sixties*, is a compact but comprehensive round-up of the years when the 'wind of change' blew so strongly.

Editorial Director
Michael Upshall

Contributors
Ingrid von Essen
Dr S P Martland
Neil Curtis

Managing Editor
Sheila Dallas

Project Editor
Neil Curtis

Produced by
Neil Curtis Publishing Services

Page layout
Richard Garratt Design

Index by
Neil Curtis

Production
Tony Ballsdon

The Sixties

1960

This was a year when Britain still believed that she had 'never had it so good'. In the midst of the postwar boom, the British prime minister Harold Macmillan, dubbed 'Supermac' by the press, had delivered economic prosperity, full employment, and a sense that Britain mattered in the world. In an attempt to bring down cold-war tensions, Macmillan arranged a summit conference between US president Eisenhower, himself and France's president de Gaulle, and the Russian leader Nikita Khruschev. The summit, held in Paris, was overshadowed by the shooting down of a US spy plane over the Soviet Union and the capture of its pilot Gary Powers. The conference collapsed when an angry Khruschev walked out on the meeting. It was an election year in the United States. The two contenders, vice president Richard Nixon and sena-tor John Kennedy, used television for the first time as a platform to debate the issues. The power of the medium was such that the more photogenic Kennedy emerged the clear victor. Though, in the November elections, he won the presidency by only a handful of votes.

Cameroon, in W Africa, becomes independent from France. Ahmadou Ahidjo is elected president.

French currency reform: the new franc is worth 100 old francs.

In the South African parliament, the new Progressive Party shocks members of other parties by calling for an end to **apartheid**.

Two divers in a bathyscaph reach the bottom of the **Mariana Trench**, E of the Mariana Islands in the NW Pacific Ocean, and discover that life exists even at a depth of 10,907 m/35,820 ft.

French Nobel prizewinning writer **Albert Camus** is killed in a car crash at 46. His works include the essay collection *Le Mythe de Sisyphe/The Myth of Sisyphus* 1942 and the novels *L'Etranger/ The Outsider* 1942 and *La Peste/The Plague* 1948.

Bahamian-born singer **Emile Ford** becomes the first black Briton to have a number-one record, with 'What Do You Want to Make Those Eyes at Me For?'

Cuba signs a $100-million **sugar-trade agreement** with USSR.

UK prime minister Harold Macmillan makes a speech in the South African parliament about the '**wind of change**' and the need to accept black nationalist aspirations.

The wind of change is blowing through this continent, and whether we like it or not, this growth of national con-sciousness is a political fact.
British prime minister **Harold Macmillan**, visiting South Africa

---

France holds its first **atomic bomb test** in the atmosphere over the Algerian part of the Sahara Desert, becoming the fourth country known to have a nuclear weapon.

In the US struggle for **civil rights**, sit-in demonstrations begin at racially segregated eating places in North Carolina.

Earthquake, tsunami, and fire destroy **Agadir**, Morocco (29 Feb); 12,000 die.

A new generation of minor tranquillizers, the **benzodiazepines** (Valium, Librium), is developed at the laboratories of Swiss pharmaceutical giant Roche.

The Broadway cast LP of Richard Rodgers and Oscar Hammerstein's musical *The Sound of Music* begins a stay of 277 weeks in the US chart.

The **Sharpeville massacre** (21 March): South African police fire at anti-apartheid demonstrators and kill 69.

The African National Congress and similar political organizations are banned in South Africa (25 March) after a civil-disobedience campaign against the **pass laws** that require the black population to carry identity documents at all times and that restrict freedom of movement.

US space probe *Pioneer 5* is launched, the first of a series to study the solar wind between the planets.

US rock-and-roll singer **Elvis Presley** returns from his stint in the US Army and begins to make the film *GI Blues*.

Scottish singer **Lonnie Donegan** has his last UK number one, 'My Old Man's a Dustman'. The skiffle music that he pioneered is soon superseded by beat music.

Togo, in W Africa, becomes independent from France.

South Korean president **Syngman Rhee** resigns, but not before protests against rigged elections (he was the only candidate) have been violently suppressed by police (127 killed).

Thousands of **East Germans**, visiting over Easter, seek asylum in West Berlin.

The UK scraps the attempt at developing an independent delivery system, **Blue Streak**, for its nuclear weapons.

Brasilia becomes the new, purpose-built capital of Brazil. The town plan is by Lucio Costa and the architect is Oscar Niemeyer.

The world's first weather satellite, *TIROS I*, is launched by the USA; *TIROS II* will follow (Nov). They send back to Earth pictures of cloud cover and are especially good for tracking storms.

English dramatist Harold Pinter's play *The Caretaker*, combining realistic dialogue with the approach of the Theatre of the Absurd, is produced in London.

US rhythm-and-blues songwriter **Bo Diddley** releases his classic song 'Roadrunner'.

A car crash on the A4 in Wiltshire kills US rocker **Eddie Cochran** and injures **Gene Vincent** (17 April); they had been touring the UK together.

A supersonic US spy plane of the **U-2** model is shot down over the USSR. The pilot, **Gary Powers** of the Central Intelligence Agency, is imprisoned (to be swapped for a US-held Soviet agent two years later). The incident causes a chill in US–Soviet relations.

British prime minister Harold Macmillan organizes a **summit conference** between the 'Big Four', President Eisenhower of the US, France's President de Gaulle, Nikita Khruschev of the Soviet Union, and himself. Khruschev demands an apology for the U-2 spy plane affair and walks out on the meeting.

Military coup in Turkey led by General Cemal Gürsel; president Celal Bayar is imprisoned and prime minister Adnan Menderes subsequently executed.

In the USSR, **Leonid Brezhnev** is appointed to the purely ceremonial post of state president.

US Civil Rights Act passed after segregationist filibuster.

The Fantastick opens off-Broadway in New York to become the world's longest-running musical. It was written by Harvey Schmidt (music) and Tom Jones (not the Welsh pop singer) (lyrics).

A renegotiated **security treaty** between Japan and the USA is ratified despite weeks of large protest demonstrations (May to June).

Soviet spacecraft *Sputnik 4* launched. It is part of a series of ten satellites, beginning 1957.

The **Kariba hydroelectric dam** on the Zambezi River in the Federation of Rhodesia and Nyasaland (from 1980 on the Zambia–Zimbabwe border) is officially opened.

Russian writer **Boris Pasternak** dies at 70. He is best known for the novel *Dr Zhivago* 1957.

The **Everly Brothers** duo reach number one in both the UK (May) and the USA (June) with their own composition 'Cathy's Clown'.

The central African **Congo** republic (Zaire) becomes independent from Belgium under President Joseph Kasavubu and prime minister Patrice Lumumba.

A **rift** develops between China and the USSR (openly from June); Soviet technical advisers are withdrawn. Soviet premier Nikita Khrushchev calls Mao Zedong a Stalinist; the Chinese leader calls Khrushchev a revisionist.

> *Politicians are the same all over. They promise to build a bridge even where there is no river.*
> **Nikita S Khrushchev**, Soviet leader, visiting the USA

English photographer Anthony Armstrong-Jones marries **Princess Margaret**.

The Jaguar car manufacturer in the UK takes over **Daimler Motor**.

English composer Benjamin Britten's opera *A Midsummer Night's Dream* opens.

English composer Lionel Bart's musical *Oliver* opens in London; it will run for 2,618 performances.

Swedish boxer **Ingemar Johansson** loses the world heavyweight title to its previous holder, **Floyd Patterson** of the USA.

Independent **Somalia**, in NE Africa, is formed by the merger of British and Italian Somaliland. The country's first president is Aden Abdullah Osman (until 1967).

Gabon, in central Africa, and Madagascar become independent from France. The first president of Madagascar is Philibert Tsiranana and of Gabon Léon M'ba (dies 1964).

Civil war breaks out between the Congolese central government and **Katanga** province (called Shaba 1963–93); it will last until 1963. Lumumba requests UN help; secretary general Dag Hammarskjöld sends UN peacekeeping troops into Katanga.

Ghana, in W Africa, becomes a republic, with Kwame Nkrumah as president, but stays within the Commonwealth.

Sirimavo Bandaranaike of Ceylon (Sri Lanka) becomes the world's first female prime minister (until 1965).

President Dwight D Eisenhower announces, with reference to **Cuba**, that the USA will not permit a government 'dominated by international Communism' to exist in the western hemisphere.

Khrushchev threatens to protect **Cuba** with rockets against any US military intervention.

Provoked by a statement by Khrushchev, Eisenhower reaffirms the **Monroe Doctrine** (that the USA will retaliate against outside intervention in the western hemisphere).

New elections are held in **South Korea**.

Aneurin Bevan, deputy leader of the British Labour Party, dies; born 1897.

'**Walk, Don't Run**' by the Ventures is the first surf instrumental and a top-ten hit in the UK and in the USA.

'**Alley Oop**' by the Hollywood Argyles is the only US number one by this studio-assembled band.

Benin (as Dahomey) in W Africa, **Burkina Faso** (as Upper Volta) in W Africa, **Central African Republic**, **Chad** in N central Africa, **Congo** in W central Africa, and **Ivory Coast** in W Africa become independent from France. Their first presidents are, respectively, Hubert Maga, Maurice Yaméogo, David Dacko,

François Tombalbaye, Abbé Youlou, and Félix Houphouët-Boigny.

Cyprus, island in the Mediterranean Sea, becomes independent with Archbishop Makarios III as president, but Britain retains its military bases there.

A right-wing military coup in **Laos** sets up a pro-Western government; civil war continues.

The satellite *Echo I* is launched by the USA. Expanding into a large sphere of aluminium foil, it reflects microwaves and will enable scientists to determine the density and composition of the outer atmosphere.

The satirical revue *Beyond the Fringe* opens at the Edinburgh Festival. It will run in London 1961–66 and launch the careers of comedians Peter Cook and Dudley Moore, playwright Alan Bennett, and director Jonathan Miller.

Life is rather like a tin of sardines – we're all of us looking for the key.
Alan Bennett, *Beyond the Fringe*

The **Shadows** have their first instrumental UK number one, 'Apache', supplanting 'Please Don't Tease' by Cliff Richard, whose backing group they are.

English beat group the **Beatles** play their first gig in Hamburg, Germany.

US singer **Tina Turner** makes her first record, with husband Ike Turner, 'A Fool in Love'.

The summer **Olympic Games** are held in Rome, Italy.

W Germans are required by E Germany to have entry permit for **E Berlin**.

Mali in NW Africa, **Niger** in NW Africa, and **Senegal** in W

Africa become independent from France. Mali's first president, Modibo Keita, imposes an authoritarian socialist system; Hamani Diori is Niger's first president; Léopold Senghor is Senegal's first president.

The Organization of Petroleum-Exporting Countries (**OPEC**) is established to co-ordinate the price and supply policies of oil-producing states.

Military coup in the **Congo** (Zaire) led by Mobutu Sese Seko. Lumumba is imprisoned, though later released, and five months later power is handed back to Kasavubu.

English suffragette **Sylvia Pankhurst** dies; born 1882.

The first **nuclear-powered aircraft carrier** is launched, the USS *Enterprise*.

Penguin Books publish D H Lawrence's novel *Lady Chatterley's Lover* in the UK and are prosecuted for obscenity (Sept–Nov); after eminent witnesses testify to the book's merit, Penguin are acquitted.

Would you allow your wife or your servant to read this book?
Mervyn Griffith-Jones, counsel for the prosecution at the trial of the publishers of *Lady Chatterley's Lover*

Traffic wardens begin to patrol the streets of London.

Premiere of English dramatist Robert Bolt's historical play *A Man for All Seasons*, starring Paul Scofield as Thomas More.

US soul singer Sam Cooke's **'Chain Gang'** is a top-ten hit.

Nigeria, W Africa, becomes independent from Britain, within the Commonwealth, as a constitutional monarchy; Alhaji Abubakar Tafawa Balewa is prime minister.

All US businesses in **Cuba** are nationalized without compensation; the USA imposes a trade embargo.

Khrushchev takes off a shoe and thumps it on his desk at the UN General Assembly when accused of Soviet imperialism in Eastern Europe.

Japanese politician **Inajirō Asanuma** is assassinated by a sword-wielding teenager for having supported the Japanese-US military treaty.

The Labour Party adopts a resolution seeking the withdrawal of US nuclear bases from the UK, and the abandonment of British **nuclear weapons**.

The USA launches its first communications satellite, *Courier IB*, for the use of the Defense Department. A radio signal beamed at it will be amplified and reflected onwards to another part of the world.

The first **electronic watch** comes on the market; it is driven by a vibrating tuning fork. Spring-driven wind-up watches will become largely a thing of the past.

The US presidential election is won by the Democratic candidate **John F Kennedy** after televised debate against Richard Nixon.

Do you realize the responsibility I carry? I'm the only person standing between Nixon and the White House.
John F Kennedy to historian Arthur M Schlesinger

Mauritania, NW Africa, becomes independent from France, with Moktar Ould Daddah as president.

The **Benelux customs union** between Luxembourg, Belgium, and the Netherlands becomes fully effective. Agreed 1944, it was a precursor of the European Union.

Military coup in **South Vietnam** fails to dislodge US-supported president Ngo Dinh Diem.

British Labour politician **Anthony Wedgwood Benn**, on inheriting the title of Viscount Stansgate, is forced to resign his seat in Parliament.

US film star **Clark Gable** dies at 59 during the making of *The Misfits*, written by Arthur Miller for Marilyn Monroe.

A good newspaper, I suppose, is a nation talking to itself.
US dramatist **Arthur Miller**

'Stay' by Maurice Williams and the Zodiacs reaches number one in the USA.

The National Front for the Liberation of South Vietnam is formed by Vietnamese communists (the **Vietcong**).

Compulsory **military service** for young men is about to end in the UK: the last call-up papers are sent out.

English director **Peter Hall** becomes the first head of the Royal Shakespeare Company (RSC), with the Aldwych Theatre, London, as its permanent base. Glen Byam Shaw has just resigned as director of the Shakespeare theatre at Stratford-upon-Avon. The RSC's first performance is John Webster's tragedy *The Duchess of Malfi*, starring Peggy Ashcroft.

South African politician **Albert Luthuli** wins Nobel Peace Prize.

The musical *Camelot* by Alan Jay Lerner and Frederick Loewe opens in New York. It stars Julie Andrews and Richard Burton, and will run for 873 performances.

US country-pop singer **Johnny Tillotson** has a UK number one with 'Poetry in Motion'.

The **Shirelles**, regarded as the first of the era's girl groups, release 'Will You Love Me Tomorrow?', which becomes a US number one and also their biggest UK hit.

The European Free Trade Association (**EFTA**) is established between Austria, Denmark, Norway, Portugal, Sweden, Switzerland, and the UK. There are no import duties between member countries.

The **Central American Common Market** (Guatemala, Honduras, El Salvador, Nicaragua) is established to encourage economic development and co-operation between member countries and to attract industrial capital.

French writer **André Malraux** becomes minister of cultural affairs (until 1969).

Exiled from South West Africa (Namibia), **Sam Nujoma** becomes the United Nations (UN) representative of SWAPO (South West Africa People's Organization).

The **Tupamaros** left-wing urban guerrilla group is formed in Montevideo, Uruguay.

West Germany's **'economic miracle'** is under way, with industrial production at 176% of the 1936 level.

British double agent **George Blake** is unmasked by a Polish defector. Blake worked for MI5 but also for the KGB.

Legal aid becomes available for divorce cases in the UK.

London slum landlord Peter Rachman gives his name to the language for unscrupulously forcing out sitting tenants (**Rachmanism**).

A **Committee of 100** breaks off from the UK Campaign for Nuclear Disarmament to advocate direct action and civil disobedience. Its most illustrious member is philosopher Bertrand Russell.

The standard **metre** is redefined as equal to 1,650,763.73 wavelengths of one of the spectral lines of an isotope of krypton. Previously it was the distance between two marks on a bar of platinum and iridium kept in special conditions of temperature and pressure at the International Bureau of Weights and Measures' laboratory in Sèvres, near Paris.

The first **laser** (acronym for <u>l</u>ight <u>a</u>mplification by <u>s</u>timulated emission of <u>r</u>adiation) is created in a US laboratory by physicist Theodore Maiman.

A plain paper **photocopier**, the Xerox 914, is introduced by the US company Xerox.

Computer typesetting is developed at the Imprimerie National, France.

The world's first **felt-tip pen** comes on the market in Japan.

Messenger RNA, a nucleic acid that acts as the template for protein synthesis in the body, is discovered by South African scientist Sidney Brenner and French biochemist François Jacob.

Chlorophyll is first synthesized, by US chemist Robert Woodward.

The Indonesian government together with the World Health Organization begins a campaign to eradicate **malaria** which, in that country, has accounted for some 120,000 deaths a year.

Haemodialysis (filtering of blood to remove waste products) is made more practicable by improvements to the kidney machine.

The **contraceptive pill** for women becomes available in the USA and tests begin in the UK.

British surgeons develop the **pacemaker** implant for patients with irregular heartbeat.

Lung cancer kills 10,000 people in England and Wales this year (compared with fewer than 250 in 1920).

The newly discovered **Mössbauer effect** (in certain conditions a nucleus can be stimulated to emit sharply defined beams of gamma rays) of atom emissions is used in the first laboratory test of Albert Einstein's general theory of relativity.

In particle physics, particles that exist for only minute fractions of a second are detected in a specially constructed bubble chamber; they are called **resonance particles**.

The first **portable television** is developed by the Japanese company Sony.

Aluminium comes into use for food and drink cans.

The **Mississippi River** is now so polluted that millions of fish die from lack of oxygen.

There is **famine in China** after failure of the Great Leap Forward programme, while the US grain surplus reaches $6 billion worth.

The first **underwater circumnavigation** of the Earth is made by US nuclear submarine *Triton*.

From this year a Soviet **nuclear-powered icebreaker** keeps open an Asia–Europe passage of 4,000 km/2,500 mi along the north coast of Siberia for 150 days a year.

The Goon Show comedy programme ends its 11-year run on BBC radio. It was the creation of Peter Sellers, Spike Milligan, and Harry Secombe.

The UK daily *News Chronicle* ceases publication. It has more than a million readers but cannot attract sufficient advertising revenue to stay afloat.

The soap opera *Coronation Street* begins in the UK.

The **cathedral** at New Norcia, near Perth, Australia, is the work of Italian architect Pier Luigi Nervi.

Dutch architect Aldo van Eyck's **Children's Home**, Amsterdam, emphasizes the relationship of the part to the whole and establishes his worldwide reputation.

Swiss artist Jean Tinguely produces, at the Museum of Modern Art in New York, a mechanical sculpture called *Homage to New York* with many moving parts and noisemakers, designed to self-destruct in front of an invited audience. This event forms a link between Dada and the happenings (mixed-media events) of the 1960s.

British sculptor Anthony Caro finds his style with the metal sculpture *24 Hours*.

US artist Ed Kienholz has an exhibition of **conceptual art** in which the purchaser can buy just the concept, or a drawing of the concept, or commission the fully executed work.

Manifeste Situationniste, the manifesto of the Situationist movement (situationists believe that moral attitudes are more important than moral rules), is published in France; its full effects are not felt until May 1968.

Irish novelist Edna O'Brien publishes her first novel, *The Country Girls*. It causes a stir in Ireland because of its sexual openness and presumed autobiographical elements.

John Barth's copious novel *The Sot-Weed Factor* is published in the USA.

Stan Barstow's novel *A Kind of Loving* realistically depicts English working-class life.

English poet John Betjeman's verse autobiography *Summoned by Bells* is published.

English poet Ted Hughes publishes the collection *Lupercal*.

Polish-US writer Isaac Bashevis Singer's novel *The Magician of Lublin* is published.

La Route des Flandres/The Flanders Road by French novelist Claude Simon is published.

US writer John Updike publishes the novel *Rabbit, Run*.

US historian William Shirer publishes *The Rise and Fall of the Third Reich*.

Clea, the last novel of British writer Laurence Durrell's Alexandria Quartet, is published.

Japanese avant-garde writer Kōbō Abe publishes *Suna no onna/ The Woman of the Dunes*, about a male teacher trapped in a sandpit with a woman; it will become the first of his novels to be translated into English.

Northern Irish-born novelist Brian Moore publishes *The Luck of Ginger Coffey*.

English children's writer Alan Garner publishes his first story *The Weirdstone of Brisingamen*, a magic adventure.

Scottish psychiatrist R D Laing publishes *The Divided Self*, a study of schizophrenia with wider cultural implications.

Italian film director Federico Fellini makes *La dolce vita*. Swedish starlet Anita Ekberg and German model Nico (later to sing with the Velvet Underground) are in the cast.

Going to the cinema is like returning to the womb; you sit there, still and meditative in the darkness, waiting for life to appear on the screen.
Federico Fellini

The comedy *The Apartment* by US film director Billy Wilder, starring Shirley MacLaine and Jack Lemmon, is released.

British-born US film director Alfred Hitchcock's *Psycho* stars Anthony Perkins.

The film *Scent of Mystery* is released in Smell-O-Vision; the technique does not catch on.

Czechoslovak director Karel Reisz, working in the UK, films the novel *Saturday Night and Sunday Morning* by Alan Sillitoe, who also wrote the screenplay; it stars Albert Finney.

Luchino Visconti's film *Rocco e i suoi fratelli/Rocco and His Brothers* is an Italian Neo-Realist epic.

Italian director Vittorio De Sica's film *Two Women* stars Sophia Loren.

René Clair becomes the first film director to be elected to the French Academy, and makes the film *Tout l'or du monde*.

US actor and director Orson Welles's London production of Eugène Ionesco's absurdist play *Rhinoceros* stars Laurence Olivier.

Irish actor, director, and dramatist Micheál MacLiammóir tours the British Isles with his one-person show *The Importance of Being Oscar* based on the life of writer and wit Oscar Wilde.

Italian director Franco Zeffirelli directs Shakespeare's *Romeo and Juliet* at the Old Vic Theatre, London, with Judi Dench as Juliet and John Stride as Romeo.

The play *Billy Liar* by Keith Waterhouse and Willis Hall, directed by Lindsay Anderson and starring Albert Finney, begins a long run in London.

US dancer and choreographer Alvin Ailey's signature piece *Revelations* enters his company's repertory.

A new **opera house opens in Salzburg**, Austria, for the annual music festival. It seats 2,160 and has the largest stage in the world. The first performance is *Der Rosenkavalier* by German composer Richard Strauss.

English composer Peter Maxwell Davies writes *O Magnum*

Mysterium for voices and orchestra, meant to be suitable for school Christmas performances.

US singer **Maria Callas** returns to La Scala, Milan, where in the next two years she will sing in revivals of such operas as *Norma* and *Medea*.

Swedish tenor **Jussi Björling** dies; born 1911. He performed earlier this year at Covent Garden Opera House, London, and the Metropolitan Opera, New York.

Premiere of *Threnody for the Victims of Hiroshima* by Polish composer Krzystof Penderecki.

Italian composer Luigi Nono writes the opera *Intolleranza*.

The **Stax record company** is founded in Memphis, Tennessee; it will become a byword for soul music.

US pop singer Chubby Checker starts a new dance craze with **'The Twist'**, previously recorded by Hank Ballard.

The year's novelty hits are **'Tie Me Kangaroo Down, Sport'** by Australian entertainer Rolf Harris and **'Itsy Bitsy Teenie Weenie Yellow Polka Dot Bikini'** by US pop singer Brian Hyland.

US pop singer **Brenda Lee** changes from rock to ballads with 'I'm Sorry', the first of her two US number-one hits this year.

US vocal group the Drifters record **'Save the Last Dance for Me'**.

Greek composer Manos Hadjidakis's title song for the film *Never on Sunday* (with Melina Mercouri) is a worldwide hit.

US golfer Arnold Palmer wins the US Open.

Lester Piggott becomes British champion jockey for the first time. He also rides the Derby winner.

1961

In 1961, people in Britain and elsewhere witnessed rapid and accelerating social, political, and cultural change. As former colonies began to achieve independence, many old European empires in Africa, the Middle and Far East, slipped into history. In 1961 Yuri Gagarin, the first astronaut, demonstrated the potential of new technologies, and old leaders, nurtured in nineteenth-century ideas, began to give way to a new generation tempered by the wars, conflicts, and experiences of the twentieth century. Nothing symbolized this change more than the coming to the United States presidency of John Fitzgerald Kennedy, the first president to be born in the twentieth century. This was also the year when tensions between the Eastern communist bloc and the West spilled over into conflict and confrontation. In the Americas, Cuba's espousal of communism was seen as a threat to the heart of the United States while, in Europe, the building of the Berlin Wall was viewed by many as a further attempt to consolidate Soviet influence at the heart of Europe.

Outgoing US president **Dwight D Eisenhower** severs diplomatic relations with Cuba.

John F Kennedy takes office (20 Jan) as the youngest-ever president of the USA.

Ask not what your country can do for you – ask what you can do for your country.
US president **John F Kennedy**, inaugural address

Coup in **El Salvador** establishes the right-wing National Conciliation Party (PCN) in power.

A campaign of civil disobedience in **Ceylon** (Sri Lanka) leads to riots.

Rwanda in central Africa becomes a republic but remains a trust territory under Belgian administration.

The overthrown prime minister of the Congo (Zaire), **Patrice Lumumba**, is murdered in the breakaway Katanga province (Jan, but not announced until Feb). The US Central Intelligence Agency (CIA) later admits responsibility.

A US Air Force bomber carrying **nuclear bombs** crashes in Goldsboro, North Carolina. The bombs do not explode but one of them breaks open on impact. Additional safety devices are subsequently installed.

The **contraceptive pill** for women becomes available in the UK.

US writer **Dashiell Hammett** dies at 66. Author of *The Maltese Falcon* 1930, he originated the hardboiled-detective school of fiction.

Rebellion begins in **Angola**, SW Africa, against Portuguese colonial rule. An estimated 20,000 Angolans are killed this year by the authorities for having nationalist sympathies.

The **Treason Trial in South Africa** ends. All 156 accused, who had been arrested in Dec 1956 for endorsing the Freedom Charter of the African National Congress (ANC), are acquitted of attempting the violent overthrow of the state. They include Nelson Mandela and Walter Sisulu.

US President Kennedy establishes the **Peace Corps** for volunteers to work in poorer countries.

A spy trial begins in the UK. The central figure is a Canadian entrepreneur, **Gordon Lonsdale**, accused of having obtained secrets from two civil servants at the Portland Underwater Weapons Establishment and passed them to the USSR.

The first **minicabs** appear on London's streets.

US artist Allan Kaprow stages *A Spring Happening* in a New

York gallery. Spectators are herded into a black tunnel and subjected to various noises while catching glimpses of performers through a slit in the wooden tunnel wall.

Death of English conductor **Thomas Beecham** at 81.

The Everly Brothers' song **'Walk Right Back'** is number one in the UK.

Sierra Leone in W Africa achieves independence from Britain within the Commonwealth.

Exiled Cuban rebels, trained and supplied by the CIA, attempt to invade Cuba at the **Bay of Pigs** (17–20 April). Of about 1,500 taking part, 1,173 are taken prisoner by the Cubans.

A military insurrection in **Algeria** by members of the Organisation de l'Armée Sécrète (OAS) is suppressed. The OAS, consisting of right-wing French soldiers and settlers, attempt by a continued terrorist campaign to delay Algerian independence.

The trial of German SS official **Adolf Eichmann** begins in Israel. He will be sentenced to death for Nazi war crimes.

The fearsome word-and-thought-defying banality of evil.
German-born US philosopher **Hannah Arendt** on the revelations during the trial of Nazi official Adolf Eichmann

---

Soviet cosmonaut **Yuri Gagarin** becomes the first person in space, orbiting the Earth just once in the spacecraft *Vostok 1* (12 April).

BBC radio terminates the programme *Children's Hour*, broadcast since 1922.

'Blue Moon' by the Marcels, a US vocal group, is number one in the UK and in the USA.

US songwriter **Bob Dylan** has his first recording session –

playing harmonica on folk singer Harry Belafonte's 'Midnight Special'.

South Africa becomes a republic, withdrawing from the Commonwealth.

In a military coup, right-wing general Park Chung-Hee seizes power in **South Korea**.

Cuban leader **Fidel Castro** offers to exchange the Bay of Pigs prisoners for 500 bulldozers, but negotiations break down.

Dominican military dictator **Rafael Trujillo Molina** is assassinated. His closest associates are deported and take with them $500 million in cash, but the rest of their assets – Trujillo owned virtually the whole island and its economic organizations – are taken over by the state. Freedom of speech and association is introduced.

The **'freedom riders'**, or civil-rights volunteers from northern states of the USA, are attacked by white segregationists in Montgomery, Alabama, and elsewhere.

US astronaut **Alan Shepard** becomes the second person and first American in space with a 15-minute hop in a Redstone rocket, the first event of the Mercury project.

New **public telephones** installed in the UK (May onwards) replace a model into which coins had to be inserted before dialling.

US film actor **Gary Cooper** dies at 60. He often played morally upright characters of few words, as in the classic western *High Noon* 1952.

The Sound of Music, a musical first produced in New York 1959, opens in London and will run until Jan 1967.

Soviet chess player **Mikhail Botvinnik** becomes world champion for the third time; he first won the title in 1948.

English football team **Tottenham Hotspur** wins the FA Cup as well as the League title.

Kuwait, a self-governing British protectorate in SW Asia, becomes fully independent, though Iraq lays claim to it.

The **Antarctic Treaty** comes into force, initially for 30 years. It places the continent under international management for peaceful scientific research, and bans nuclear explosions and the disposal of nuclear waste in the Antarctic.

Nelson Mandela announces that he will remain in hiding inside South Africa to lead the struggle for equal rights.

Swiss psychiatrist **Carl Gustav Jung** dies at 85.

Russian dancer **Rudolph Nureyev** defects to the West during a visit to Paris with the Kirov Ballet.

Clean-cut US teen idol **Ricky Nelson** has a US number one (UK number two) with the double A-side 'Hello, Mary Lou' / 'Travelin' Man'.

Michael Ramsey is elevated from archbishop of York to archbishop of Canterbury.

US President Kennedy, citing the **'worldwide Soviet threat'**, announces increased resources for the military: an extra $3.4 million and 217,000 soldiers.

US writer **Ernest Hemingway** commits suicide at 61.

The musical *Stop the World, I Want to Get Off* opens in London; it stars Anthony Newley, who cowrote it with Leslie Bricusse.

The border between East and West Berlin is sealed with barbed wire (13 Aug) by East German security forces, and Soviet forces then begin building the **Berlin Wall** to prevent the escape of unwilling inhabitants of East Germany to the Western zone.

The UK formally applies for membership of the **European Economic Community**.

> *I think it is about time we pulled our finger out.*
> **Prince Philip**, Duke of Edinburgh, addressing entrepreneurs in London

Elections are held in **Kenya**, E Africa, still a British colony, but the winning party, Kenya Africa National Union, does not form a government until the release from prison of its leader, Jomo Kenyatta.

The **Marvelettes** release their first record (on Tamla Motown), 'Please, Mr Postman', later to be covered by the Beatles.

UN secretary general **Dag Hammarskjöld** dies in a plane crash (18 Sept) while trying to mediate in the Congo–Katanga conflict.

The **United Arab Republic** (Egypt and Syria) breaks up after a military coup in Syria asserts independence.

First conference of the **nonaligned movement** held in Belgrade, Yugoslavia. Member countries oppose colonialism, imperialism, and the dominance of the superpowers.

Out of more than 15,000 demonstrators, 850 are arrested at a rally in Trafalgar Square, London, against **nuclear weapons**. Among them are jazz singer and writer George Melly and actress Vanessa Redgrave. Philosopher Bertrand Russell was already jailed the previous week.

Irish writer Samuel Beckett's play *Happy Days* has its premiere off-Broadway in New York.

US pop singer **Bobby Vee** has a number one in both the UK and the USA with 'Take Good Care of My Baby', his biggest hit.

The volcanic island of **Tristan da Cunha** in the S Atlantic erupts and the few hundred inhabitants are evacuated; they will return 1963.

France gives up its naval base in **Bizerta**, Tunisia, after clashes with Tunisian nationalists.

The **Sino-Soviet split** deepens when Chinese prime minister Zhou Enlai walks out of a Communist Party congress in Moscow.

The USSR continues **nuclear-weapons testing** with a 57-megaton bomb in the Novaya Zemlya area.

The Labour Party affirms support for US **nuclear bases** in Britain, reversing its position of the previous year.

Welsh-born British painter **Augustus John** dies at 83.

The **twist** is a worldwide dance craze, with 45 different twist records out in France alone.

US soul singer Ray Charles's **'Hit the Road, Jack'** is a US number one pop single.

Burmese diplomat **U Thant** succeeds Dag Hammarskjöld as secretary general of the UN.

Several cities in the USSR named after former dictator Joseph Stalin change their names (Stalingrad reverts to Volgograd, Stalinsk becomes Novokuznetsk) as part of Soviet leader Nikita Khrushchev's **de-Stalinization programme**; Stalin's body is removed from the mausoleum in Red Square, Moscow.

An employee in the UK Foreign Office, **John Vassall**, is convicted of having spied for the USSR; he had been blackmailed into it.

A West German doctor notices a correlation between birth defects and use of the drug **thalidomide**, a sedative.

Andorra by Swiss dramatist Max Frisch has its premiere in Zurich. The play, about anti-Semitism, will become an international success.

Frank Loesser's musical *How to Succeed in Business Without*

Really Trying opens on Broadway, New York, and will run for 1,417 performances.

Tanganyika (now forms the mainland of Tanzania) in E Africa achieves independence within the Commonwealth; the prime minister is Julius Nyerere.

The secession of **Katanga** is officially ended with a cease-fire in the Congo.

The UN representative in the Congo, Irish diplomat **Conor Cruise O'Brien**, is forced to resign.

Castro declares **Cuba** a one-party communist state on Marxist-Leninist lines.

Umkhonto we Sizwe, the military wing of the ANC, is formed in South Africa.

Enver Hoxha, the communist dictator of Albania, breaks off relations with the USSR and withdraws from the East-bloc economic organization Comecon.

The USA sends 400 additional troops ('military advisers') to Saigon, beginning the escalation of the **Vietnam War**.

French political writer **Frantz Fanon** dies at 36 in the USA; he will be best remembered for the posthumously published *Les Damnés de la terre/The Wretched of the Earth* 1964.

The **John Coltrane Quartet** is recorded *Live at the Village Vanguard* in New York and will become a legendary name in jazz.

The Tokens' US number one **'The Lion Sleeps Tonight'** is an adaptation of a Zulu song, 'Mbube'.

Helen Shapiro, at 14, is voted the year's Best Female British Singer after having number-one hits with 'You Don't Know' and 'Walking Back to Happiness'.

The **Organization for Economic Co-operation and Develop-**

ment supersedes the Organization for European Economic Co-operation. It co-ordinates the economic policy strategies of the 24 industrialized member nations.

Revolt by **Kurds** begins in the province of Kirkuk, NE Iraq. Aspirations to an autonomous Kurdish state lead to almost continual revolt in the 1960s and 1970s.

The Portuguese territories of **Daman** and **Goa** on the W coast of India are annexed by India.

The president of Brazil, **Janio Quadros**, resigns after only seven months; the army restricts the power of his successor, João Goulart, suspecting him of left-wing leanings.

Hassan II comes to the throne of Morocco.

Amnesty International is founded in the UK to work for the release of prisoners of conscience worldwide. The organization will succeed in reducing the number of political prisoners over the next 30 years.

Belize City in British Honduras is destroyed by a hurricane.

British diplomat **George Blake** is sentenced to 42 years' imprisonment for passing secrets to the USSR.

Pelican crossings are introduced in London.

Meteorologist Edward Lorenz discovers a mathematical system with chaotic behaviour, leading to a new branch of mathematics: **chaos theory**.

Steven Hofstein in the USA designs the field-effect transistor used in integrated circuits (**silicon chips**).

The **intrauterine device (IUD)**, or loop, is developed as a contraceptive in the USA.

US biochemists Marshall Nirenberg and Severo Ochoa determine the chemical nature of the **genetic code**.

Austrian physicist **Erwin Schrödinger** dies. He was born 1887, and advanced the study of wave mechanics.

Element 103, **lawrencium**, is first produced, albeit only a few atoms of it.

A microwave beam is directed at the planet **Venus** and reflected back, enabling scientists to measure the distance more accurately than before.

The USA launches the first **nuclear-powered satellite**.

A variety of **tomato** that can be machine-picked without damage is developed at the University of California and becomes popular with growers.

US multinational company IBM introduces the **Selectric golf-ball typewriter**, designed by Eliot Noyes.

The **Kenwood Chef** kitchen appliance, by British designer Kenneth Grange, is first produced.

A study group presents the British government with plans for a double-bore **Channel tunnel**.

An Antarctic expedition (to 1962) discovers the Bentley Trench, which suggests that there may be an **Atlantic–Pacific link** beneath the continent.

The **medieval Swedish warship** *Wasa* is raised intact from Stockholm harbour, to be preserved in a museum.

The **E-type Jaguar**, perhaps the archetypal 1960s car, is launched.

Dag Hammarskjöld is awarded the Nobel Peace Prize, the first time it has been awarded posthumously

The US **Marvel Comics** Group launches *The Fantastic Four* starting a trend with superheroes who have human failings. Marvel comics soon become a 1960s cult among teenagers and students.

Penguin Books begin to put pictures on their covers.

The **Archigram** group of radical English architects and designers is formed; their ideas are experimental and polemical, and they advocate flexible technological solutions.

Death of US architect **Eero Saarinen**, born in Finland 1910. His TWA terminal at Kennedy Airport, New York, shows imaginative use of concrete (completed 1962).

The **Lillington Road housing estate** designed by British partnership Darbourne and Darke is built in Pimlico, London. With its red brick and enclosed courtyards, it is a successful example of low-cost urban housing.

The **Chase Manhattan Bank skyscraper** by the US architect firm of Skidmore, Owens & Merrill is built in the Wall Street district of New York.

The **London Zoo birdcage** in Regent's Park is built, designed by Cedric Price with Lord Snowdon and Frank Newby. Price is one of the most visionary avant-garde British architects of the period.

The **Park Hill housing estate** is built in Sheffield, England; the architects are Lynn, Smith, and Nicklin under Wormersley. It is an example of the architectural style Brutalism (developed by Alison and Peter Smithson) in its organization and use of materials.

The **Pirelli Building** is built in Milan, designed by Italian architect Gio Ponti.

Bulgarian-born artist **Christo** conceives of wrapping larger and larger objects as temporary installations. From *Dockside Packages*, Cologne, West Germany, he will go on to wrap buildings and natural features.

French sculptor **César** begins using crushed car bodies, as in *The Yellow Buick*.

The Store by Swedish-born US artist Claes Oldenburg is an installation in a New York art gallery where the artist sells papier-mâché food and other objects for two months as if it were a shop.

Soviet poet Yevgeni Yevtushenko publishes the poem *Babi Yar*, about a Nazi massacre of more than 100,000 people in Ukraine during World War II. He is denounced by Soviet authorities for implicit criticism of Stalinism.

US writer Joseph Heller publishes his first novel, *Catch-22*, based on his experience of World War II.

There was only one catch and that was Catch-22, which specified that a concern for one's own safety in the face of dangers that were real and immediate was the process of a rational mind.
Joseph Heller, *Catch-22*

British writer V S Naipaul publishes the novel *A House for Mr Biswas*, set in his native Trinidad.

The Pride of Miss Jean Brodie by Scottish novelist Muriel Spark is published; it is set in an Edinburgh girls' school in the 1930s.

The Long Revolution, written by Welsh cultural critic Raymond Williams, predicts Britain's social problems of later decades and sets out ways to avert them (which are not adopted).

Riders in the Chariot by Australian novelist Patrick White is published, an allegorical novel about four outcast mystics.

Two long stories by cult writer J D Salinger are collected in the USA as *Franny and Zooey*.

English writer Angus Wilson publishes the novel *The Old Men at the Zoo*, set in the London of a hypothetical 1970.

US Beat Generation poet Allen Ginsberg publishes *Kaddish and Other Poems*.

R D Laing publishes *The Self and Others*.

True guilt is guilt at the obligation one owes to oneself to be oneself. False guilt is guilt felt at not being what other people feel one ought to be or assume that one is.
Scottish psychiatrist **R D Laing**, *The Self and Others*

French philosopher Michel Foucault publishes one of his major works, *Histoire de la folie/Madness and Civilization*.

English novelist Graham Greene publishes *A Burnt-Out Case*, set in the Congo.

English novelist Richard Hughes publishes *The Fox in the Attic*, set in the 1920s.

Japanese novelist Sawako Ariyoshi's *Hanoaka Seishu no tsuma/ The Doctor's Wife* deals with the plight of women in the traditional Japanese household.

English writer Lucy M Boston publishes the children's novel *A Stranger at Green Knowe*, in which a gorilla escapes from London Zoo.

French film director François Truffaut makes *Jules et Jim* with Jeanne Moreau in the female lead.

Belgian director Agnes Varda makes the film *Cléo de 5 à 7*.

Audrey Hepburn stars in Blake Edwards's film *Breakfast at Tiffany's*, whose theme song 'Moon River' becomes a hit in many versions.

English actress Rita Tushingham stars in Tony Richardson's film *A Taste of Honey*, based on Shelagh Delaney's play.

The French New Wave film *L'Année dernière à Marienbad/ Last Year in Marienbad* by Alain Resnais is released. The matchstick game that recurs in the film puzzles audiences for the rest of the year.

US composer Leonard Bernstein's musical *West Side Story* is filmed in Hollywood with choreography by Jerome Robbins.

Paul Newman and Jackie Gleason star in the Hollywood film *The Hustler*, directed by Robert Rossen.

The play *Luther* by English dramatist John Osborne has its premiere in Paris, in an English Stage Company production with Albert Finney in the title role.

US dramatist Jack Gelber's 1959 play *The Connection* causes controversy when brought to the UK by the Living Theatre company.

The cantata *Sutter's Gold* by British composer Alexander Goehr provokes outrage at its premiere in Leeds, Yorkshire, by its Modernism.

Influenced by US avant-garde composer John Cage, British composer Cornelius Cardew writes *Octet* 'for any instruments'.

Austrian composer György Ligeti achieves international prominence with the orchestral work *Atmosphères*.

Hungarian-born British conductor **Georg Solti** becomes musical director at Covent Garden Opera House, London.

English conductor **Colin Davis** becomes musical director at Sadler's Wells, London (until 1965).

Canadian soprano **Teresa Stratas** sings the part of Mimi in Giacomo Puccini's opera *La Bohème* at Covent Garden, London.

The Dave Brubeck Quartet's jazz instrumental in fi÷¢ time, **'Take Five'**, is an international hit single.

US singer **Roy Orbison** records his melodramatic hits 'Running Scared' and 'Crying'.

1962

During 1962 Britain was still enjoying the fruits of the postwar boom. With full employment, record levels of domestic consumption, and sustained growth in the economy, it seemed an optimistic time, particularly for the young. With a television in almost every home, the benefits of a consumer society were apparent, and when, for the first time, the satellite *Telstar* broadcast programmes directly from the United States, it seemed as if science fiction had become a reality. Abroad, in sharp contrast to the domestic scene, the bloody conflict in the Congo, brought nightly into the home through the medium of television, demonstrated that it was easier to acquire than to dispose of empires. Meanwhile, the cold war between East and West reached new levels of confrontation when, in October 1962, the Soviet Union erected in Cuba nuclear-tipped missiles pointed at the United States; it provoked a crisis that nearly plunged the world into a nuclear war.

Western Samoa, in SW Pacific Ocean, achieves independence within the Commonwealth, having been a trust territory administered by New Zealand. The first prime minister is Fiame Mata Afa Mulinu'u.

Indonesia lays claim to **Irian Jaya** (W New Guinea), a Dutch colonial possession.

Fighting resumes in the Congo (Zaire) between the central government and the breakaway **Katanga** republic.

The **Organisation de l'Armée Secrète (OAS)** takes its terrorist bomb campaign against Algerian independence to Paris.

The **Beatles** audition for Decca and are rejected.

Groups of guitars are on the way out, Mr Epstein – you really should stick to selling records in Liverpool.
Decca A & R person **Dick Rowe** to the Beatles' manager

The USA imposes an embargo on nearly all trade with **Cuba**.

John Glenn in *Friendship 7* becomes the first American to orbit the Earth; two other US astronauts make orbits later in the year.

The last of the great transatlantic passenger liners, **SS *France***, makes its first voyage from Le Havre to New York.

The *Sunday Times* is the first British newspaper to introduce a colour supplement.

British satirical magazine ***Private Eye*** is launched and receives financing from comedian Peter Cook.

Premiere in Zurich of Swiss dramatist Friedrich Dürrenmatt's play ***Die Physiker/The Physicists***. The Royal Shakespeare Company will perform it in London 1963.

German-born US conductor **Bruno Walter** dies at 85.

The **twist** is still energetically danced: Chubby Checker's 'Let's Twist Again' is number one in the UK, and 'Peppermint Twist' by Joey Dee and the Starlites is number one in the USA (Jan–March).

US-supported South Vietnamese forces launch an offensive against **Vietcong** guerrillas.

In a UK by-election, the Liberals win the 'safe' Conservative seat of **Orpington**, a London suburb. It shows dissatisfaction with the government and gives the Liberals hope of gaining support nationwide.

Georges Pompidou becomes prime minister of France, continuing the conservative government under president Charles de Gaulle.

The USA tests **nuclear weapons** on Christmas Island (now Kiritimati) in the South Pacific.

A demonstration in Hyde Park, London, against **nuclear weapons** draws a crowd of 150,000.

The *Radcliffe Report* advocates banning communists from the UK civil service.

The UK's first satellite, *Ariel*, is launched by the USA.

Arnold Wesker's play *Chips with Everything*, illustrating class conflict in Britain, opens at the Royal Court Theatre, London.

Geneva Agreement establishes a three-party government in **Laos**, where there has been civil war since independence 1954, but fighting continues between the communist Pathet Lao and the US-backed right wing.

Two **Orient Express** train services from Paris to Istanbul are discontinued because of competition from air travel.

Trolley buses cease to run in London.

Coventry Cathedral, England, is consecrated. It was designed by Scottish architect Basil Spence and incorporates the ruins of the old cathedral, destroyed in World War II.

US Abstract Expressionist painter **Franz Kline** dies at 51.

Romanian-born dramatist Eugène Ionesco's play *Le Roi se meurt/ Exit the King* is given its first production in Paris. It will be staged at the Royal Court in London 1963, starring Alec Guinness.

Frelimo (acronym for Front for the Liberation of Mozambique) is established in Mozambique, SE Africa, to fight for liberation from Portuguese colonial rule.

Mongolia joins Comecon, the East-bloc economic organization.

The UK's first legal **casino** opens in Brighton.

The **Pilkington Committee** on UK broadcasting reports that television 'will in time do much to worsen the moral climate of the country'.

French avant-garde artist **Yves Klein** dies at 34. His works include conceptual art, mixed-media events, monochrome paintings, and neo-Dadaist gestures.

The **first album chart** in the UK is introduced by the *New Musical Express*.

Algeria, in N Africa, achieves independence from France after a referendum in which 6 million vote for independence and 16,500 against.

Rwanda and **Burundi** in central Africa achieve independence from Belgium. Rwanda's first president is Grégoire Kayibanda and Burundi is a monarchy under King Mwambutsa IV.

British Conservative politician Reginald Maudling becomes chancellor of the Exchequer, replacing John Selwyn Lloyd, whose policy of wage restraint to control inflation forces his resignation. Altogether seven cabinet members are replaced in what becomes known as the **Night of the Long Knives**, prompted by a Conservative by-election loss.

The **Commonwealth Immigration Act** restricts emigration to the UK.

The **National Economic Development Council (Neddy)** is set up in the UK for economic consultation between government, management, and trade unions.

US communications satellite *Telstar* is launched, and sends the first live television transmission between the USA and Europe. The instrumental 'Telstar' by the **Tornadoes**, produced by Joe Meek, makes them the first British group to top the US chart.

US Nobel prizewinning novelist **William Faulkner** dies at 64; his works include *The Sound and the Fury* 1929 and *Light in August* 1932.

The **Chichester Festival Theatre** opens in Sussex, England. Laurence Olivier is its head (until 1965) and stars, with Michael Redgrave, in Anton Chekhov's *Uncle Vanya* in the first season.

Australian athlete **Dawn Fraser** swims 100 m in less than a minute, the first woman to do so.

The **West Indies Federation** dissolves when **Jamaica**, and **Trinidad and Tobago**, become independent within the Commonwealth. Jamaica's first prime minister is Alexander Bustamante (until 1967) and Trinidad and Tobago's is Eric Williams.

In South Africa, **Nelson Mandela**, commander of Umkonto we Sizwe, the military wing of the African National Congress, is captured and imprisoned.

An OAS extremist attempts to assassinate French president **de Gaulle**.

A tunnel is completed under **Mont Blanc** in the French Alps.

US film star **Marilyn Monroe** dies of a drugs overdose (5 Aug) at 36.

Ahmed Ben Bella, who has led the National Liberation Front since 1952, is appointed prime minister of Algeria.

The University of Mississippi is forced to admit its first black student, **James Meredith**, but federal troops are needed to guard him from racists for the whole academic year.

Colour television broadcasting gradually begins in the USA (from Sept).

The UK's **ITV network** is completed with the addition of Channel Television and Wales West and North (Teledu Cymru).

The **Four Seasons'** high harmony vocals on 'Sherry' give them the first of many US number-one hits.

US boxer **Sonny Liston** knocks out **Floyd Patterson** to become world heavyweight champion.

Cuban missile crisis: confrontation between the USA and the USSR over the installation of Soviet missiles on Cuba. After a US naval blockade of Cuba amid worldwide fears of nuclear war, Soviet premier Nikita Khrushchev agrees to have the missiles removed, and US missiles in Turkey are removed as a trade-off.

We're eyeball to eyeball, and the other fellow just blinked.
US secretary of state **Dean Rusk** on the Cuban missile crisis

---

Uganda, E Africa, achieves independence from Britain, within the Commonwealth, with Milton Obote as prime minister.

Border clashes between Chinese and Indian forces.

The publisher of West German magazine *Der Spiegel* is arrested for having criticized the country's armed forces. The result is a debate about **press freedom** and the resignation of six ministers (Nov), including defence minister Franz Josef Strauss.

US dramatist Edward Albee's most realistic play, ***Who's Afraid of Virginia Woolf?***, has its premiere in New York; it will open in London 1964.

The Beatles' first single **'Love Me Do'** is released (5 Oct); it enters the UK top 30 for one week. Eventually it will sell a million copies worldwide.

US record producer and songwriter **Phil Spector**, a millionaire at 21, becomes the youngest ever record-company owner when he buys out his partner.

US folk trio **Peter, Paul and Mary** release their eponymous first LP. It will spend six weeks at number one in the US pop chart.

The **Second Vatican Council** is summoned by Pope John XXIII.

Eritrea, which has been a federated region of Ethiopia since 1952, is annexed by the central government, losing its self-governing status, and a resistance movement begins.

Eleanor Roosevelt, who was US First Lady 1933–45 and helped draw up the United Nations Declaration of Human Rights, dies at 78.

US Republican politician **Richard Nixon** loses the election for governor of California.

You won't have Nixon to kick around any more.
US politician **Richard Nixon** to the press after losing the election for governor of California

---

US Democrat politician **Edward Kennedy** is elected senator for Massachusetts despite admitting earlier this year that he once had a proxy sit his exams at Harvard University.

Danish physicist **Niels Bohr**, who helped establish the validity of quantum theory, dies at 77.

UK Foreign Office clerk **John Vassall** is convicted of having handed over secrets to the USSR.

Phil Spector's girl group the **Crystals** have a US number one with 'He's a Rebel'.

Tanganyika, in E Africa, becomes a republic with Julius Nyerere as president, but remains within the Commonwealth.

Nassau Agreement: the USA agrees to sell Polaris missiles to the UK for launching British-built nuclear warheads from British submarines.

US space probe *Mariner 2* is the first to fly past Venus; it confirms the existence of solar wind and measures the Venusian temperature.

The first successful **kidney transplant** is carried out, at Leeds General Infirmary, Yorkshire, England.

Smog in London kills 60 people in three days.

Most of those who took part in the ill-fated **Bay of Pigs** invasion attempt 1961 are ransomed from Cuba for $53 million in food and medicine.

Ne Win seizes power in a military coup in Burma (Myanmar). His 'Burmese Way to Socialism' programme will bring the country into serious economic decline.

The existence of the US **National Security Agency** (established 1952) is for the first time officially acknowledged; it is the largest US intelligence agency, and intercepts telecommunications.

The **Dominican Republic** holds its first free elections. Juan Bosch, founder of the left-wing Dominican Revolutionary Party, becomes president.

The **Sandinista National Liberation Front (FSLN)** is formed in Nicaragua to overthrow the US-backed right-wing regime of the Somoza family.

The European Economic Community initiates the **Common Agricultural Policy**. It is based on a price-support system to stabilize markets, which will lead to farmers being subsidized for overproduction.

Costa Rica joins the **Central American Common Market**.

French president **de Gaulle** visits West Germany for the first time since World War II, marking the resumption of friendly relations between the two countries.

A military junta is installed by a coup in **Ecuador**.

Great Britain has lost an empire and not yet found a role.
US politician **Dean Acheson**

The **sultan of Brunei** begins rule by decree; the UK remains responsible for Brunei's external affairs.

Crown Prince Faisal becomes prime minister of Saudi Arabia for the second time.

The **Central African Republic** becomes a one-party state, the only permitted political organization being the Movement for the Social Evolution of Black Africa (MESAN) founded by president David Dacko's uncle Barthélémy Boganda in the 1950s.

The **FNLA (National Front for the Liberation of Angola)** is the second nationalist movement to be formed in Angola (a Portuguese colony in SW Africa).

Anatoly Dobrynin becomes Soviet ambassador to the USA.

John Foster Dulles International Airport outside Washington DC opens; it is the first civil airport specifically designed for jet planes, and the terminal is designed by Finnish-born architect Eero Saarinen.

The US **Lear jet** is introduced; it will become the most popular private jet plane.

British physicist Brian Josephson predicts the properties of a supercurrent through a tunnel barrier (the **Josephson effect**). This leads to the development of the **Josephson junction**, a device used to speed the passage of signals in complex integrated circuits.

Benoit Mandelbrot in the USA invents **fractal images**, programming a computer to repeat the same mathematical pattern over and over again. The result is a motif that repeats indefinitely, each time smaller. This is one of the most decorative and readily comprehensible aspects of **chaos theory**.

The first **X-ray source** in outer space is discovered in the constellation Scorpius.

By using microwave beams, two US astronomers establish the rotational period of **Venus** at about 250 days (later confirmed to be 243 days) and find that the planet rotates from east to west, in the opposite direction from all other planets in the Solar System.

The **intelligence of dolphins** is investigated by US scientist John Lilly.

UK-born Canadian chemist Neil Bartlett becomes the first to make a **compound of noble gases** when he combines xenon and fluorine.

The first **light-emitting diodes (LEDs)** are produced. They will become common in electronic displays, and are made of semiconductor material that glows when electricity is passed through it.

Polaroid colour film is introduced. It produces prints in 60 seconds.

Lasers are used in eye surgery for the first time.

Soft contact lenses are invented by Czechoslovak Otto Wichterle.

A **vaccine against German measles (rubella)** is developed in the USA. It is a mild virus disease, common in childhood, but can cause foetal damage if caught by pregnant women.

The sedative **thalidomide** is banned from sale in the UK, but not before more than 5,000 babies worldwide have been born with missing or deformed limbs because their mothers took the drug in early pregnancy.

The first **sugar-free soft drink** comes on the US market (Diet-Rite Cola).

The **ring-pull** is invented for aluminium beverage cans.

France and the UK agree to develop a supersonic airliner; it will become known as the **Concorde**.

The **Ford Cortina** will become Britain's most popular car.

The first industrial **robots** are installed by US car manufacturer General Motors.

The **Esalen Institute** is founded in California, starting a boom in psychotherapy and self-improvement.

Smoking and Health, a report by the Royal College of Physicians, first highlights the physical damage caused by smoking.

The realistic police drama series *Z Cars* begins on BBC television; it will run until 1965.

Johnny Carson begins several decades of hosting *The Tonight Show* on US television.

Wolfsburg Cultural Centre near Brunswick, West Germany, is completed (begun 1959); the architect is Alvar Aalto of Finland.

English artist Graham Sutherland designs a **tapestry for Coventry Cathedral**, West Midlands.

The **Fluxus group** of artists hold a show in London called Festival of Misfits. Events include Canadian performance artist Robin Page, wearing a silver helmet, kicking a guitar round the block.

The publication of *Silent Spring* by US naturalist Rachel Carson draws public attention to the cumulative effects of pesticides on the environment.

Canadian communications theorist Marshall McLuhan coins the phrase **'the global village'** in his book *The Gutenberg Galaxy*.

US writer Katherine Anne Porter publishes her only novel, the allegorical *Ship of Fools*.

Russian-born US novelist Vladimir Nabokov publishes the novel *Pale Fire*.

US writer Ken Kesey's first novel, *One Flew Over the Cuckoo's Nest*, uses a mental hospital as a metaphor for society.

Soviet writer Alexander Solzhenitsyn's novel *One Day in the Life of Ivan Denisovich* exposes conditions in labour camps under Stalin.

US poet **e e cummings** dies; born 1894.

English novelist J G Ballard makes his breakthrough with ***The Drowned World***, depicting a future disaster.

US cult writer Philip K Dick wins the Hugo award for ***The Man in the High Castle***, set in a hypothetical world in which the Nazis won World War II.

Russian poet Anna Akhmatova finishes ***Poem Without a Hero*** (begun 1940).

Scottish poet **Hugh McDiarmid** publishes his *Collected Poems*.

German-born Swiss writer **Hermann Hesse** dies; born 1877. His theme of spiritual searching was important throughout the 1960s.

British novelist Doris Lessing publishes ***The Golden Notebook***, an influential feminist work.

US writer James Baldwin publishes the novel ***Another Country***.

English poet **Roy Fuller** publishes his *Collected Poems*.

A Clockwork Orange by English novelist Anthony Burgess depicts a future dominated by violent youth gangs.

English poet **Stevie Smith** publishes her *Selected Poems*. She does many readings in the 1960s, in person and on radio.

US novelist Alison Lurie publishes her first novel ***Love and Friendship***.

English writer Aldous Huxley publishes the Utopian novel ***Island***.

English writer and critic Penelope Mortimer publishes the novel ***The Pumpkin Eater***.

English writer Philippa Pearce publishes the children's novel ***A Dog So Small***.

English writer Pauline Clarke publishes ***The Twelve and the Genii***, a children's novel.

English film director David Lean's epic *Lawrence of Arabia* stars Peter O'Toole in the title role.

Spanish Surrealist Luis Buñuel makes the disturbing film *El angel exterminador/The Exterminating Angel*.

US director John Ford's film *The Man Who Shot Liberty Valance*, starring John Wayne, is a classic Western.

US actor Paul Newman stars in the film *Hud*, directed by Martin Ritt and based on a Larry McMurtry novel.

Bette Davis and Joan Crawford star in the Hollywood horror film *Whatever Happened to Baby Jane?*

French New Wave director Jean-Luc Godard makes *Vivre sa Vie*, starring Anna Karina.

The great Japanese director Yasujirō Ozu makes his last film, *Samma no aji/An Autumn Afternoon*.

Polish director Roman Polanski makes his first film, the steely *Noz w wodzie/Knife in the Water*.

Japanese director Kon Ichikawa makes *Yukinojo henge/An Actor's Revenge*, a theatrical film about a female impersonator.

French filmmaker Robert Bresson makes *Le Procès de Jeanne d'Arc/The Trial of Joan of Arc*.

US actor Robert Mitchum stars in *Cape Fear*.

'The name is Bond, **James Bond**.' Sean Connery, in *Dr No*, becomes the first film actor to embody Ian Fleming's creation, agent 007.

English director **Peter Brook** becomes codirector, with **Peter Hall** and **Michel Saint-Denis**, of the Royal Shakespeare Company, where his first production is *King Lear* in Stratford-upon-Avon, starring Paul Scofield.

US choreographer Glen Tetley's ballet *Pierrot Lunaire*, in which he is one of the three dancers, opens in New York. Later in the year, he joins the Nederlands Dans Theater.

Ballet dancers **Rudolph Nureyev** and **Margot Fonteyn** first appear together, in *Giselle*. Their partnership at the Royal Ballet will become legendary.

Austrian violinist **Fritz Kreisler** dies. Born 1875, he was one of the earliest recording artists of classical music.

English composer Michael Tippett writes *Songs for Ariel*.

English composer Nicholas Maw writes *Scenes and Arias* for three female singers and orchestra.

Scottish Opera is founded by Alexander Gibson, conductor of the Scottish National Orchestra.

US crooner Tony Bennett records **'I Left My Heart in San Francisco'**.

US saxophone player Stan Getz and guitarist Charlie Byrd introduce **bossa nova**, a Latin dance rhythm, on the hit LP *Jazz Samba*.

French model **Françoise Hardy** makes her debut as a singer and songwriter with 'Tout les Garçons et les filles', and becomes an international star at 18.

French fashion designer **Yves Saint-Laurent** shows his first collection under his own name.

Brazilian footballer **Pelé** leads his country to victory in the soccer World Cup.

English motor-racing driver **Graham Hill** becomes Formula 1 world champion for the first time, for BRM.

Australian **Rod Laver** wins the grand slam in tennis.

US golfer **Arnold Palmer** loses the US Open to newcomer **Jack Nicklaus** but wins the British Open.

1963

This was a year of great contrasts. One was the wholly unexpected emergence in Britain of a new form of youth culture, which expressed itself in the music of the Beatles (whose first record appeared in 1963). It was a hedonistic culture, spawning with it new ideas concerning music, the arts, clothes, hairstyles, and sexual liberation. These ideas spread quickly across Britain, and then around the world. Most of all it shocked the older generation, unable to comprehend, control, or accept what was happening. Politically, it was a bad year for Conservative prime minister Harold Macmillan. The Profumo scandal, the French veto on Britain's Common Market application, a deteriorating economy and ill-health forced his resignation. However, 1963 is mainly remembered for the tragedy of President Kennedy's assassination, with its bitter feelings of optimistic hopes dashed and innocence lost. This was also the year of Martin Luther King's march on Washington DC to claim equal rights for all, regardless of race. All in all, by the end of 1963, with so many certainties evaporating, many people in Britain were feeling confused, anxious, and concerned about the future.

Hugh Gaitskell dies; born 1906. Harold Wilson succeeds him as UK Labour Party leader.

The Britain that is going to be forged in the white heat of this revolution will be no place for restrictive practices or outdated methods on either side of industry.
Labour Party leader **Harold Wilson** addressing the party conference

---

The attempted secession of **Katanga** province in the Congo (Zaire) ends; Moise Tshombe, the Katangan leader, goes into exile.

Britain's application to join the **European Economic Community** is vetoed by France.

British double agent **Kim Philby** flees to the USSR.

Exceptionally **cold weather in Britain** (Dec 1962–Feb 1963) causes pipes to freeze and disrupts public transport; London has 60 deaths from smog.

A **BBC ruling** that comedy shows must not mention sex, politics, royalty, or religion is rescinded.

US poet **Robert Frost** dies at 88. Such poems as 'Stopping by Woods on a Snowy Evening' are much anthologized.

In Iraq, President **Abdul Karim Kassem** is killed in a joint Ba'athist-military coup led by Col Salem Aref and backed by the US Central Intelligence Agency. Some 5,000 alleged communists are also killed.

ZAPU (Zimbabwe African People's Union) leader **Joshua Nkomo** returns to Southern Rhodesia (now Zimbabwe) from brief exile and is imprisoned.

Italy nationalizes its **power stations**.

US poet **Sylvia Plath** commits suicide in London. Her *Collected Poems* 1981 will win a Pulitzer Prize.

The play *Der Stellvertreter/The Deputy* by German dramatist Rolf Hochhuth has its premiere in Berlin. It creates controversy by criticizing Pope Pius XII's compliant attitude to the Nazis during World War II.

The musical *Half a Sixpence* opens in London, starring Tommy Steele. It is based on the novel *Kipps* by H G Wells and will run for 677 performances.

Military coup in **Guatemala**: President Carlos Castillo Armas is assassinated; Col Enrique Peralta becomes president.

The first **metal tennis racket** is produced by French shirtmaker and former tennis champion René Lacoste.

The Beatles release their first LP, *Please Please Me* (22 March).

The UK begins to sell military supplies to the new Iraqi regime (March–April onwards), which uses the arms against the **Kurds**.

US country singer **Patsy Cline** dies at 30 in a plane crash in Tennessee, on her way back to Nashville after playing a benefit in Kansas City. She is remembered for such hits as 'Walkin' After Midnight' and 'I Fall to Pieces'.

The Easter protest march from **Aldermaston** to London draws 70,000 demonstrators opposed to nuclear weapons.

The countercultural *Oz* magazine begins publication in Australia.

The **Organization of African Unity** is established to improve political, economic, and cultural co-operation in Africa.

A **cyclone** in East Pakistan (Bangladesh) makes 500,000 people homeless and kills 10,000.

US blues guitarist **Elmore James** dies at 45; he is best remembered for his version of the blues standard 'Dust My Broom' and his bottleneck style of playing had great influence on rock guitarists.

Tigran Petrosian becomes the new world chess master after defeating his fellow Soviet Mikhail Botvinnik.

US president **John F Kennedy visits West Berlin** and tells the inhabitants that he identifies with them.

All free men, wherever they may live, are citizens of Berlin. And therefore I take pride in the words: Ich bin ein Berliner.
US president **John F Kennedy**, visiting West Berlin, Germany

---

David Ben-Gurion resigns as prime minister of Israel and is succeeded by **Levi Eshkol**.

A **Vietnamese Buddhist monk sets himself on fire** in protest against official South Vietnamese policies that adversely affect Buddhists; the US-supported government is mainly Roman Catholic. Many other monks will also kill themselves in this way.

US Congress passes an act requiring **equal pay for women** for equal work.

Governor **George Wallace** of Alabama attempts to use the National Guard to prevent two black students from entering the University of Alabama.

President Kennedy introduces **civil-rights legislation**.

UK war minister **John Profumo** resigns because he lied to Parliament in denying his affair with call girl **Christine Keeler**, who has also been sleeping with a Soviet naval attaché.

Valentina Tereshkova in *Vostok 6* (USSR) becomes the **first woman in space**.

English rhythm-and-blues group the Rolling Stones make their first record, a cover of Chuck Berry's **'Come On'**.

Death of **Pope John XXIII**; he is succeeded by **Paul VI**.

Australian tennis player **Margaret Court** wins the Wimbledon singles title for the first time.

British and US intelligence agencies finance and encourage a general strike and rioting against the left-wing government of **British Guiana**. The UK sends troops and imposes its own terms for the colony's eventual independence.

The Yugoslavian city of **Skopje** is destroyed by an earthquake.

The **Peerage Act** becomes law, enabling hereditary British peers to disclaim their peerage for their lifetime.

The first geostationary satellite, *Syncom 2*, is launched by the USA.

Britain's **first hovercraft passenger service** opens at Rhyl, Wales.

David Hockney makes his first visit to California this summer. His fascination with painting water dates from this time.

ZANU (Zimbabwe African National Union) is formed as an offshoot of ZAPU; Robert Mugabe is one of its leaders.

The **hot-line** special telephone link between the US and Soviet heads of state becomes operational.

The United Nations (UN) Security Council **embargoes arms sales** to South Africa.

Martin Luther King addresses his **'I have a dream'** speech to 200,000 demonstrators who have marched on Washington DC to demand racial equality (28 Aug).

I have a dream that my four little children will one day live in a nation where they will not be judged by the colour of their skin but by the content of their character.
US civil-rights leader **Martin Luther King**, addressing demonstrators in Washington DC

Crop failures in China and in the Kazakhstan and Ukraine republics of the USSR cause both countries to buy grain from Canada.

The **Great Train Robbery** (8 Aug): a gang steals about £2.5 million, mainly in cash, from a mail train in Buckinghamshire, England.

Launch of *Ready Steady Go!* weekly pop programme on British television.

French painter and Cubist pioneer **Georges Braque** dies at 81.

The **Federation of Malaysia**, SE Asia, is formed, with Tunku Abdul Rahman as prime minister.

The US state of **Alabama** is forced to begin to desegregate public schools. Terrorist bomb attack on black Baptist churchgoers in Birmingham, Alabama (15 Sept), triggers race riots.

Military coup in **Dominican Republic** deposes elected left-wing president Juan Bosch.

The UK vetoes a UN Security Council resolution calling for universal suffrage in **Rhodesia** and early independence.

The **Fylingdales** early warning radar station in N Yorkshire, England, becomes operational. It is linked with similar stations in Greenland and Alaska to give a four-minute warning of nuclear attack.

The **American Express** credit card is launched in the UK; it was first introduced 1958 in the USA.

Nigeria becomes a republic; its first president is Nnamdi Azikiwe.

Nationalist leader **Ahmed Ben Bella** is elected the first president of Algeria.

Konrad Adenauer, 87, retires as chancellor of West Germany; his successor is economics minister **Ludwig Erhard**, 84.

In consequence of the Profumo scandal, **Harold Macmillan resigns** from the leadership of the Conservative Party; his successor is foreign secretary **Lord Home**.

He is used to dealing with estate workers. I cannot see how anyone can say he is out of touch.
Lady Caroline Douglas-Home on her father's becoming prime minister

French writer and film director **Jean Cocteau** dies; born 1889, he was a leading figure in European Modernism.

Britain's **National Theatre** company is established under the directorship of Laurence Olivier and temporarily based at the Old Vic, London. The opening production is Shakespeare's *Hamlet*.

US dramatist Neil Simon's play ***Barefoot in the Park*** opens in New York for a run of 1,502 performances. Robert Redford is among the cast.

Edith Piaf, French cabaret singer remembered for 'Je ne regrette rien', dies at 47.

US President **John F Kennedy is assassinated** in Dallas, Texas (22 Nov). He is succeeded by vice president Lyndon B Johnson.

The ostensible assassin of President Kennedy, **Lee Harvey Oswald**, is shot dead in police custody (24 Nov), live on television, by Jack Ruby, a Dallas club owner.

US-supported military coup in **South Vietnam**; President Diem is assassinated.

Volcanic activity off the S coast of Iceland creates a new island, named **Surtsey**.

The first **push-button telephones** are introduced in the USA.

Viking remains are found in Canada, dating from about 1000.

English writer **Aldous Huxley** dies; born 1894. Best known for the dystopian novel *Brave New World*, he explored the effects of psychedelic drugs in his last years in California.

Beatlemania breaks out in the autumn. The group gives its first Royal Variety Performance, and Lennon and McCartney are proclaimed by the *Times* music critic 'the greatest composers since Beethoven'.

*On the next number, would those in the cheap seats clap
their hands? The rest of you rattle your jewellery.*
John Lennon, of the Beatles, to the audience at the Royal
Variety Performance

Kenya, E Africa, under President Jomo Kenyatta, and Zanzibar
become independent states within the Commonwealth.

Federation of **Rhodesia** (now Zambia and Zimbabwe) and
Nyasaland (now Malawi) dissolved.

In **Cyprus**, Turks set up their own government in the north and
fighting breaks out between the Turkish and Greek communities.

In South Africa, a trial of 11 African National Congress leaders
begins, known as the **Rivonia Trial** after the place where they
were arrested – all but Nelson Mandela, who was already in jail
but is tried with the others.

The irreverent current-affairs programme *That Was the Week That
Was* is axed after nine months, but political satire has arrived on
UK television.

Death of **C S Lewis** at 65, British author of the Narnia stories for
children.

German Neo-Classical composer **Paul Hindemith** dies at 68.

US jazz and rhythm-and-blues singer **Dinah Washington** dies at
39. She was known as 'queen of the blues' before turning to jazz.

Nuclear Test Ban Treaty signed by the USA, the USSR, and the
UK, agreeing to test nuclear weapons only underground. France
will carry out a further 37 atmospheric tests, and China has yet to
begin atmospheric testing.

In **Chad**, a revolt against the government begins in the Muslim
north, backed by Libya.

Constitutional monarchy is established in **Afghanistan**.

Irian Jaya, the western part of New Guinea, is ceded by the Netherlands to Indonesia.

Liberal Party is returned to power in Canada: **Lester Pearson** becomes prime minister.

Syrian government formed, mainly from the **Ba'ath Party**, in place of military rule. Ba'ath is a pan-Arab nationalist party.

The Indian state of **Nagaland** is established in response to demands for self-government, but Naga liberationist guerrilla activity continues.

Tunisia becomes a one-party state.

South Africa introduces a law under which anyone suspected of subversion can be held without charge or trial for any number of consecutive 90-day periods.

Typhoons in Japan cause serious damage to crops.

US singer and actor **Paul Robeson** causes controversy in the USA by visiting the USSR as a communist.

Alcatraz prison in San Francisco Bay, California, is closed down. The island fortress, a military prison 1886–1934 and then a federal penitentiary, was supposedly escape-proof because of strong tidal currents in the bay.

British Labour politician **Tony Benn**, having disclaimed his peerage, is re-elected to the House of Commons.

The British House of Lords is the British Outer Mongolia for retired politicians.
Labour politician **Tony Benn** on renouncing his peerage

Members of the Committee of 100 peace organization break into the British government's **emergency bunker** near Maidenhead, Berkshire, S England, drawing unwelcome attention to its existence.

The first **quasar** (small distant starlike object – from quasi-stellar object) is discovered. It was identified by radio waves it emitted, but most quasars are radio-quiet. Quasars are billions of light years away.

The **Arecibo radio telescope** in Puerto Rico is completed, the largest of its kind in the world; it is operated by Cornell University, USA.

The discovery of seafloor sediments with **reverse magnetization** confirms both the theory of seafloor spreading (growth of the ocean crust away from midocean ridges) and the periodic reversal of the Earth's magnetic field.

The **Corvette Sting Ray** is one of the most stylish cars of the decade.

The first **electronic calculator** is built by the US Bell Punch Company.

The first **minicomputer** is built by Digital Equipment (DEC) in the USA.

The UN Food and Agriculture Organization begins a campaign to increase **world food production** by 140% by 1985. Strains of various cereal crops are introduced that in some places will double yields, but with a far greater increase in fertilizer and pesticide use, with some undesirable side effects.

British archaeologist Walter Emery pioneers rescue archaeology at **Abu Simbel**, Egypt, before the site is flooded by the Aswan Dam.

Carbon fibre is invented at the Royal Aircraft Establishment in Farnborough, Hampshire, England.

Cibachrome photographic paper and chemicals for printing directly from transparencies become commercially available.

The *Beeching Report* on the railways is published in the UK: a committee chaired by Lord Beeching advocates the closure of many rural lines.

Traffic in Towns, the report of the Buchanan Committee commissioned by the UK Ministry of Transport, recommends improved public transport and traffic-free neighbourhoods; the report is largely ignored by the ministry.

Polypropylene **stacking chairs** designed by Robin Day (UK).

Kodak Instamatic cameras that can be loaded with film cartridges are introduced.

The **Weight Watchers** slimming organization is founded in New York.

Children's science-fiction serial *Dr Who* begins on British television. The title role is played by William Hartnell.

The ban on **high-rise buildings in Tokyo**, Japan, is lifted and the city's first tower block is built.

Roy Lichtenstein paints *Whaam!*, a Pop-art work in comic-strip style.

Italian Conceptual artist **Piero Manzoni** dies; born 1933. He painted single continuous brushstrokes on long rolls of paper.

German artist Joseph Beuys creates the performance piece *How to Explain Pictures to a Dead Hare*, in which he sits holding a dead hare and talking to it, his face covered in gold leaf.

South Korean video artist Nam June Paik creates *An Exposition of Music* in Wuppertal, West Germany.

English poets Adrian Henri and Roger McGough stage some of the UK's first **'happenings'** (mixed-media events) in Liverpool.

There is a **Festival of Happenings** at US sculptor George Segal's farm in New York State.

Prague has a **happening** called *Short Carting Exhibition* created by Czechoslovak artist Milan Knížák.

Honest to God by John Robinson, bishop of Woolwich, causes controversy on publication by challenging traditional Christian beliefs.

US novelist Thomas Pynchon publishes his first novel *V*.

English novelist John Le Carré's first book *The Spy Who Came in from the Cold* heralds a wave of disillusioned spy fiction.

US writer and critic John Updike publishes the novel *The Centaur*.

Yukio Mishima's novel *Gogo no eiko/The Sailor Who Fell from Grace with the Sea* is published in Japan.

New Zealand novelist Janet Frame publishes *Scented Gardens for the Blind*.

British writer Len Deighton publishes the spy thriller *The Ipcress File*.

US novelist Mary McCarthy's semiautobiographical *The Group* becomes a best seller.

First British publication of a work by US avant-garde novelist William Burroughs, *Dead Fingers Talk*.

US feminist Betty Friedan publishes *The Feminine Mystique*. It draws attention to the limitations of the housewife and homemaker role imposed on US women since the end of World War II.

US writer James Baldwin publishes autobiographical essays in *The Fire Next Time*.

German writer Günter Grass publishes the novel *Hundejahre/Dog Years*.

US writer Kurt Vonnegut publishes the characteristically quirky novel *Cat's Cradle*.

Ivy Compton-Burnett's *A God and His Gifts* is the last of her novels to be published in her lifetime.

The title of English writer and scientist C P Snow's novel *The Corridors of Power* adds a cliché to the language.

Nigerian writer Wole Soyinka writes the play *The Lion and the Jewel*.

Czech dissident Václav Havel writes the play *The Garden Party*.

English novelist Margaret Drabble publishes her first novel *A Summer Bird-Cage*.

Peruvian novelist Mario Vargas Llosa publishes *La ciudad y los perros/The Time of the Hero*.

Historian E P Thompson publishes *The Making of the English Working Class*, shifting the historical focus from the governing to the governed.

US illustrator Maurice Sendak creates the children's picture book *Where the Wild Things Are*.

US writer Joan Aiken publishes her first novel for children, *The Wolves of Willoughby Chase*.

British writer Clive King publishes the children's novel *Stig of the Dump*.

US film director Joseph Losey, working in the UK, makes *The Servant* from a script by Harold Pinter and starring Dirk Bogarde.

Italian director Federico Fellini's semiautobiographical film *Otto e mezzo/8½* is released.

The historical Hollywood epic *Cleopatra*, starring Elizabeth Taylor and Richard Burton, is directed by Joseph L Mankiewicz.

English director Tony Richardson makes the film *Tom Jones*, based on Henry Fielding's novel.

Italian director Luchino Visconti films Giuseppe di Lampedusa's novel *Il gattopardo/The Leopard*.

French New Wave film director Jean-Luc Godard makes *Le Mépris/Contempt* with Brigitte Bardot and Fritz Lang.

English director Lindsay Anderson films David Storey's novel *This Sporting Life*.

Swedish director Ingmar Bergman makes the film *Tystnaden/The Silence*. It is the last part of a trilogy and its theme, according to Bergman, is the silence of God.

French film director Jacques Demy makes the musical *Les Parapluies de Cherbourg*.

Jeanne Moreau stars in Jacques Demy's film *La Baie des Anges/ Bay of Angels*.

Delphine Seyrig stars in *Muriel* by French film director Alain Resnais.

French director Louis Malle makes the film *Feu follet/The Fire Within*.

British pop singer Cliff Richard stars in the musical film *Summer Holiday*.

US film comedian Jerry Lewis stars in *The Nutty Professor*. His films are particularly popular in France.

The **Living Theatre** anarchist performance collective moves from the USA to Europe, where their influence will be felt for the rest of the decade.

The **Traverse Theatre** is founded in Edinburgh.

For the Royal Ballet, dancers Margot Fonteyn and Rudolph

Nureyev create the title roles in Frederick Ashton's ballet *Marguerite and Armand*.

I dance to please myself. If you try to please everybody, there is no originality.
Rudolf Nureyev

US artist **Robert Rauschenberg** presents a dance piece in New York in which the performers are on roller skates and wear parachutes.

Italian avant-garde composer Luciano Berio writes *Passaggio*; he settles in the USA this year.

Death of French composer **Francis Poulenc**; born 1899.

English composer Richard Rodney Bennett writes *The Mines of Sulphur* for Sadler's Wells Opera, London.

Dmitry Shostakovich's opera *Lady Macbeth of Mezensk*, banned by Soviet authorities 1936, is produced in a revised version as *Katerina Ismailova*.

Australian composer Malcolm Williamson writes the opera *Our Man in Havana*.

Italian tenor **Luciano Pavarotti** makes his first appearance at the Covent Garden Opera House, London, singing the part of Rodolfo in Giacomo Puccini's *La Bohème*.

Welsh soprano **Gwyneth Jones** gives her first performance at Covent Garden.

Folk and protest songs are popular in the USA; Bob Dylan's **'Blowin' in the Wind'** is a hit for vocal group Peter, Paul and Mary.

At the age of 12, **Stevie Wonder** tops the US pop single and album charts simultaneously with 'Fingertips Part 2' and *Little Stevie*

Wonder. Other Motown hitmakers this year include Mary Wells, the Miracles, and Martha and the Vandellas ('Heatwave').

US record producer Phil Spector invades the top ten with **'Da Do Ron Ron'** by the Crystals and 'Be My Baby' by the Ronettes.

US country singer Johnny Cash has one of his biggest hits, **'Ring of Fire'**.

British singer **Dusty Springfield** begins her solo career with the top-ten hit 'I Only Want to Be with You'.

Vocal **surf music** is in the US charts with the Beach Boys' 'Surfin' USA' and Jan and Dean's 'Surf City'.

The classic version of the song **'Louie, Louie'** by the Kingsmen is released; accused of obscenity, the record is found by the US authorities to be 'unintelligible at any speed'.

The song 'Dominique' is a worldwide hit for the **Singing Nun**, a Belgian who will leave her convent 1966.

Popular US folk singer **Joan Baez** champions the newcomer **Bob Dylan**.

Welsh torch singer Shirley Bassey records **'I (Who Have Nothing)'**.

British comedy combo **Freddie and the Dreamers** becomes popular on television.

British fashion designer **Mary Quant** launches her mass-produced range.

British model **Jean Shrimpton**, 'the Shrimp', becomes the world's favourite cover star.

Gillette Cup (later NatWest Trophy) cricket championship is first held. It is an annual event in the UK.

1964

In 1964, the young people of Britain went wild over the Beatles, their music, their hairstyles, and their clothes. The young were more affluent and more assertive than any previous generation had been. They were also making their own mark on British society, and daring the world to follow them. They began to assert their economic power, making an early impact on the clothing industry by discarding suits in favour of casual clothing, in particular, blue jeans. The phenomenon of Beatlemania provided a welcome diversion for Britain, in the midst of what proved to be a six-month General Election campaign. This was 'time-for-a-change' year in Britain as Harold Wilson's Labour Party was returned to office, with a tiny parliamentary majority. In sharp contrast, Lyndon Johnson (Kennedy's successor) won the United States presidential elections by a landslide.

British troops are sent to **Kenya**, **Tanganyika**, and **Uganda** at those countries' governments' request to suppress army uprisings.

US surgeon general issues a report linking **cigarette smoking** to lung cancer and other diseases.

Top of the Pops begins on BBC 1.

US dramatist Arthur Miller's play *After the Fall*, based on his marriage to Marilyn Monroe, opens in New York.

The musical *Hello, Dolly!* opens on Broadway in New York, starring Carol Channing, and will run for 2,844 performances. Music and lyrics are by Jerry Herman.

The **Rolling Stones** tour Britain with US vocal group the Ronettes.

Pope Paul VI visits Jerusalem, where he meets the patriarch of the Orthodox Church.

President **Kwame Nkrumah** proclaims Ghana a one-party state and aligns himself with the communist bloc.

The first **£10-notes** since World War II are issued by the Bank of England.

English dramatist Peter Shaffer's historical epic *The Royal Hunt of the Sun* has its premiere in London.

The **Beatles** play their first US concerts and are watched by 74 million television viewers on the *Ed Sullivan Show*. By March, the Beatles are said to account for 60% of the US singles market.

US singer Betty Everett is the first person to have a hit with **'The Shoop Shoop Song (It's in His Kiss)'**.

US boxer **Cassius Clay** becomes world heavyweight champion by defeating Sonny Liston. Having joined the Black Muslim sect, he then changes his name to Muhammad Ali.

Float like a butterfly, sting like a bee.
US boxer **Cassius Clay** describing his tactics

Bloodless military **coup in Brazil** (March–April); all political parties banned. This was triggered by an attempt by the president to redistribute federal land to those who had none.

US president Lyndon B Johnson declares **'national war on poverty'**.

United Nations Conference on Trade and Development begins in Geneva; UNCTAD will become a permanent UN agency.

US black nationalist leader **Malcolm X** breaks away from the Black Muslims.

The **abolition of retail-price maintenance** in the UK accelerates the decline of corner shops and the growth of supermarket chains.

There are two problems in my life. The political ones are insoluble and the economic ones are incomprehensible.
UK prime minister **Alec Douglas-Home**

The **St Bernard Tunnel** through the Swiss Alps opens.

Radio Caroline begins broadcasting, the first pirate radio station to challenge the BBC's monopoly in the UK.

US cabaret singer Barbra Streisand stars in the Broadway musical *Funny Girl* by Jule Styne and Bob Merrill.

For the first time, the **UK top ten** is made up of only British records.

Zanzibar, after less than six months of independence, merges with Tanganyika to form **Tanzania**.

Rhodesian Front white-supremacist party leader Ian Smith becomes prime minister, elected by the white minority of some 250,000; the black population of more than 5 million have no vote in Rhodesia.

A UN peacekeeping force is sent to **Cyprus** to keep Greeks and Turks apart.

Elections held to the new **Greater London Council**; Labour victorious.

BBC 2 television begins broadcasting.

Motown Records release Mary Wells's biggest hit, **'My Guy'**, written by Smokey Robinson.

Jamaica gives the world the first ska hit, Millie's **'My Boy Lollipop'**.

India's first prime minister, **Jawaharlal Nehru**, dies in office at 76.

South Africa extends the **apartheid laws**.

Background microwave radiation in outer space is detected by US scientists, corroborating the Big Bang theory for the origin of the Universe. It also indicates that the average temperature of the Universe is 3° above absolute zero.

Moise Tshombe, who led the failed Katanga secession, returns to the Congo (Zaire) from exile and is appointed prime minister. The last UN peacekeeping forces leave the country.

The **Rivonia Trial** ends in South Africa. Nelson Mandela, Walter Sisulu, and six others are sentenced to life imprisonment.

Three **civil-rights workers are murdered** by racists in Mississippi (June; bodies not found until Aug).

English dramatist Joe Orton's black comedy *Entertaining Mr Sloane* has its premiere in London.

The Rolling Stones record **'It's All Over Now'** in Chess Studios, Chicago, Illinois.

Nyasaland, SE Africa, achieves independence from Britain, within the Commonwealth, under the name of Malawi. Hastings Banda is its first head of government.

US **Civil Rights Act** becomes law.

Race riots in New York.

The first Beatles film is released, *A Hard Day's Night*, directed by Richard Lester.

Julie Andrews plays the title role in the Disney musical film *Mary Poppins*.

South Africa is banned from participating in the Olympic Games.

Race riots in Philadelphia, Pennsylvania.

Malta, island in the Mediterranean, achieves independence from Britain, within the Commonwealth.

Tonkin Gulf Incident: two US destroyers claim to have been fired on by North Vietnamese patrol boats (2 Aug) in international waters; the US retaliates with air raids on North Vietnam.

The **Tonkin Gulf Resolution** passed by Congress (7 Aug) gives the US president a free hand with the escalation of the Vietnam War.

We are not about to send American boys 10,000 miles away from home to do what Asian boys ought to be doing for themselves.
US president **Lyndon Johnson**, speech at Akron University, Ohio

---

Indonesian paratroops land in **Malaysia**. Indonesia regards Malaysia as a US puppet state and has, since 1963, been supporting guerrillas opposed to the federation.

The *Warren Commission Report* on the assassination of US president Kennedy is released. It states that Lee Harvey Oswald was solely responsible and there was no conspiracy.

Britain begins a search for **North Sea oil and gas**.

The **road bridge across the Firth of Forth** in Scotland, from South Queensferry, West Lothian, to Inverkeithing, Fife, is opened.

The musical *Fiddler on the Roof* opens on Broadway in New York, starring Zero Mostel, and will run for 3,242 performances. It will open in London 1967.

US comedian **Harpo Marx**, the silent Marx Brother, dies at 70.

Soviet premier **Nikita Khrushchev** is ousted by the Central Committee. A collective, conservative leadership assumes power, with

Leonid Brezhnev as Communist Party general secretary and **Alexei Kosygin** as prime minister.

Northern Rhodesia, S central Africa, achieves independence from Britain, within the Commonwealth, under the name of Zambia. Its first president is Kenneth Kaunda.

China tests its first **nuclear weapon**.

A civilian **coup in Sudan** overthrows military ruler F I Abboud. A coalition government attempts unsuccessfully to end the civil war between north and south.

General election in the UK: Labour wins a majority of 4 seats and forms a government (15 Oct) led by Harold Wilson.

The UK government accepts the recommendation of the **Robbins Committee** to double the number of university places to 218,000 by 1974 (390,000 places in all higher education).

Japan's **Shinkansen** comes into service between Osaka and Tokyo. Also called the bullet train, it is the fastest in the world to date at 210 kph/130 mph.

Canada adopts a **new flag** design that shows a maple leaf.

Japanese architect **Kenzo Tange** has designed several of the arenas for Olympic Games held in Tokyo.

US songwriter **Cole Porter** dies at 74. He wrote witty, sophisticated songs and many musical comedies.

Motown group the Supremes' **'Baby Love'** begins 13 weeks in the US chart.

Kenya, E Africa, achieves full independence from Britain, within the Commonwealth, with Jomo Kenyatta as president.

King Saud of Saudi Arabia is forced to abdicate; he is succeeded by his brother Faisal.

In US presidential elections, the incumbent Democrat **Johnson** enjoys a record victory over the far-right Republican Barry Goldwater.

> *Extremism in the defence of liberty is no vice. And let me remind you also that moderation in the pursuit of justice is no virtue.*
> US right-wing politician **Barry Goldwater** on accepting the Republican nomination for president

The city of **Venice is flooded** when the water in the lagoon rises 1.8 m/6 ft. Flooding is common in Venice but usually less severe.

The **Verrazano Narrows Bridge** between Brooklyn and Staten Island in New York is the world's longest single-span suspension bridge when it opens.

The alleged **'Boston Strangler'** serial killer Albert Henry DeSalvo is arrested in the USA.

Free Speech Movement begins at the Berkeley campus of the University of California. More than 732 sit-in demonstrators are arrested.

Radio London pirate station begins broadcasting outside British territorial waters.

German avant-garde composer **Karlheinz Stockhausen** finishes *Momente*, and *Mikrophonie I* has its premiere.

US producer Phil Spector releases **'You've Lost That Lovin' Feelin''** sung by the Righteous Brothers.

US soul singer **Sam Cooke** is shot dead in a motel brawl.

Papa Doc (François Duvalier), the right-wing dictator of Haiti since 1957, proclaims himself president for life.

A military **coup in Bolivia** is led by the vice president, General René Barrientos, deposing Victor Paz Estenssoro.

Palestine Liberation Organization (PLO) formed in Beirut, Lebanon, to bring about an independent Arab state of Palestine.

Japan signs a contract for **iron ore** from Australia that will provide its steel industry with 65 million tonnes by 1980, much of which will be made into cars.

Mods and rockers have fights on the seafront in resort towns, especially in SE England. This becomes a 1960s bank-holiday ritual.

The **topless bathing suit** is designed by Californian Rudi Gernreich, but an attempt to create a fashion for topless dresses is doomed by climate and aesthetics.

In particle physics, the existence of the **quark** is established by US physicist Murray Gell-Mann, and the charmed quark is postulated by US physicist Sheldon Lee Glashow. The quark (the name is borrowed from a word in James Joyce's *Finnegan's Wake*) is one of the fundamental constituents of matter.

Element 104 is produced by Soviet and by US physicists and is called kurchatovium by the former and **rutherfordium** by the latter.

The US car manufacturer **Studebaker–Packard** closes down.

Ford introduces the **Mustang** car.

The **Dansette** record player comes on the market at 18 guineas (£18 18s) in the UK.

Robert Moog develops the **electronic music synthesizer** (not sold commercially until 1966).

US space probe *Mariner 4* sends back pictures of Mars.

New Zealand biologist William Hamilton pioneers the concept of

inclusive fitness, paving the way for sociobiology.

The **IBM 360** is the first office computer to incorporate transistors and use magnetic tape; IBM is a US technology giant.

The computer language **BASIC** is devised in the USA.

Malaria has been almost entirely eradicated on Java. At the beginning of the Indonesian campaign 1960 it was the cause of 120,000 deaths a uncle.

The synthetic opiate **methadone** comes into use for treating heroin addicts.

The British and French ministers of transport agree on construction of the **Channel Tunnel**.

Death of German-born US physicist **James Franck**; born 1882. He worked on the atomic bomb during World War II but tried to prevent its use against Japanese cities.

The **baby boom** peaks in the UK, with a total fertility rate of 2.94.

The first **self-assembly furniture** is sold; it is made of cardboard.

English designer Terence Conran opens the first **Habitat** shop in the Fulham Road, London; Habitat will make its mark on the decade's interiors.

The Man from UNCLE spy series begins on US television.

The football television programme *Match of the Day* begins on BBC 1.

On BBC radio, the evening **Third Programme** is augmented by a daytime music programme.

Schoolteacher **Mary Whitehouse** launches a campaign to 'clean up' British television; her vociferous objections to sex and profanity will be heard for the next 30 years.

The **Economist Building** in London, by Alison and Peter Smithson, is completed. They represent the New Brutalist school of architecture.

Centre Point by Richard Seifert is completed in London. Although remaining empty for many years, this office block made its developer, Harry Hyams, a millionaire.

Lincoln Center, New York, by US architects Philip Johnson, Wallace Harrison, and Max Ambrovitz is opened. It is strongly criticized on both aesthetic and practical grounds.

The sculpture *The State Hospital* by US artist Edward Kienholz has two life-size figures in bunk beds, the upper enclosed in a thought bubble; their heads are goldfish bowls complete with fish.

English sculptor Henry Moore creates *Atom Piece*.

Canadian pundit Marshall McLuhan's book *Understanding Media* contains the catchphrase 'the medium is the message'.

The medium is the message. This is merely to say that the personal and social consequences of any medium . . . result from the new scale that is introduced into our affairs by each extension of ourselves or by any new technology.
Canadian information theorist **Marshall McLuhan**, *Understanding Media*

US novelist Saul Bellow publishes *Herzog*.

English poet Philip Larkin publishes the collection *The Whitsun Weddings*.

German political philosopher Herbert Marcuse's book *One-Dimensional Man* points out the totalitarian tendencies of Western society.

US writer **Flannery O'Connor** dies at 39. She is best known for her short stories and the novel *Wise Blood*.

English novelist Angus Wilson publishes *Late Call*.

Belgian-born French anthropologist Claude Lévi-Strauss publishes the first volume of his *Mythologiques/Mythologies*.

English novelist Christopher Isherwood publishes *A Single Man*.

Irish novelist Elizabeth Bowen publishes *The Little Girls*.

US poet Robert Lowell publishes the collection *For the Union Dead*.

US novelist J P Donleavy publishes *A Singular Man*.

Come Back, Dr Caligari is the first collection from quirky US short-story writer Donald Barthelme.

English writer A S Byatt publishes her first novel *The Shadow of a Sun*.

English novelist William Golding publishes *The Spire*.

US writer Norman Mailer publishes the novel *An American Dream*.

British writer Roald Dahl publishes the best-selling children's book *Charlie and the Chocolate Factory*.

English writer Leon Garfield publishes the first of many historical adventures for children, *Jack Holborn*.

English novelist William Mayne publishes the children's novel *Sand*.

US writer Louise Fitzhugh publishes the children's novel *Harriet the Spy*.

Stanley Kubrick makes the film *Dr Strangelove*, written by Terry Southern, about the possibility of nuclear war.

Italian director Michelangelo Antonioni makes his first colour film, *Il deserto rosso/The Red Desert*, starring Monica Vitti.

The James Bond film *Goldfinger*, with a score by English composer John Barry and title track sung by Shirley Bassey, is a great commercial success.

US actor Clint Eastwood stars in Italian director Sergio Leone's *A Fistful of Dollars*, one of a series of spaghetti Westerns.

French New Wave director Jean-Luc Godard makes the film *Une Femme mariée*.

The musical *My Fair Lady* is filmed with Audrey Hepburn and Rex Harrison.

Anthony Quinn stars as *Zorba the Greek*, in a film directed by Michael Cacoyannis.

English comedian Peter Sellers stars as the bumbling Inspector Clouseau in the *Pink Panther*, the first of five films.

Italian director Pier Paolo Pasolini makes the biblical film *The Gospel According to St Matthew*.

Death of **Peter Lorre**, Hungarian character actor who appeared in the classic Hollywood films *Casablanca* and *The Maltese Falcon*; born 1904.

US film director Joseph Losey, working in the UK, makes *King and Country* with Dirk Bogarde.

Italian director Bernardo Bertolucci makes the film *Prima della rivoluzione/Before the Revolution*.

Peter Brook produces Peter Weiss's play *Marat/Sade* in London as part of a Theatre of Cruelty season.

Premiere in London of John Osborne's play *Inadmissible Evidence*, starring Nicol Williamson.

The Irish Abbey Theatre company from Dublin takes part in London's first **World Theatre Season** with two plays by Sean O'Casey.

Irish dramatist **Brendan Behan** dies; born 1923. His autobiography *Borstal Boy* was published 1958.

English choreographer Frederick Ashton creates the ballet *The Dream*.

English composer Benjamin Britten writes *Curlew River* with William Plomer (libretto), a work for church performance.

Finnish baritone **Tom Krause** creates the role of Jason in Austrian-born US composer Ernst Krenek's opera *Der Goldene Bock* in Hamburg, West Germany.

US record producer George Shadow Morton launches girl group the **Shangri-Las** with the songs 'Remember (Walkin' in the Sand)' and 'Leader of the Pack'.

Liverpool group the **Searchers** have a big hit with their cover of 'Needles and Pins'.

Jamaican group the **Wailers** is formed by 19-year-old Bob Marley. They will be international superstars in the 1970s.

'The Girl from Ipanema' is a worldwide hit, sung by Astrud Gilberto with Stan Getz on saxophone.

South African pop musician **Manfred Mann** and his English group have an international hit with 'Do Wah Diddy Diddy'.

Motown Records' **Martha and the Vandellas** have a big hit with 'Dancing in the Street'.

British hair stylist **Vidal Sassoon** introduces the short, geometric haircut.

British car and speedboat enthusiast Donald Campbell breaks the **world land and water speed records** in Australia. The new records are (land) 648.7 kph/403.1 mph and (water) 444.57 kph/ 276.3 mph.

1965

This year saw the death of Sir Winston Churchill, Britain's last great Victorian. Also in 1965, Southern Rhodesia's racist white settler government, in an attempt to frustrate moves towards African rule, declared their independence. In retaliation, Britain imposed economic sanctions on the illegal regime. By 1965, the prosperous certainties of postwar Britain were rapidly fading, as the growth in Britain's economy began to slow, revealing a chronic balance-of-payments deficit and an overvalued currency. Meanwhile, young men in Britain began to grow their hair, and girls started wearing miniskirts, to the astonishment of their elders. In the United States, President Johnson began to pour conscript American armies into South Vietnam, in an attempt to prevent a communist takeover by the North.

Military **coup in South Vietnam**.

US president Lyndon B Johnson announces his programme of social and economic reform for a **'Great Society'**. Most of the funds will, in the event, be spent on the Vietnam War.

British Conservative politician **Winston Churchill** dies at 91 and is given a state funeral.

The Gambia, W Africa, achieves independence from Britain, within the Commonwealth, with David Jawara as prime minister.

Motown Records in the USA release the Temptations' **'My Girl'**.

USA begins **bombing raids** on North Vietnam.

US black nationalist leader **Malcolm X** is assassinated in New York by Black Muslim opponents.

The prime minister of the Irish Republic, **Sean Lemass**, goes to Belfast for a meeting with the Northern Irish prime minister, **Terence O'Neill**. It is the first time leaders of the two governments have met on Irish soil since partition of Ireland 1921.

The Rolling Stones release their first original single, **'The Last Time'**.

Australian runner **Ron Clarke** sets two new 5,000-m records.

Nicolae Ceauşescu comes to power in Romania on the death of Gheorghe Gheorghiu-Dej.

The USA admits to having used **chemical weapons in Vietnam**.

US civil-rights campaigner **Martin Luther King Jr** leads a march from Selma to Montgomery, Alabama. The demonstrators are attacked by state police and racists and have to be protected by 3,000 members of the federal National Guard.

In a UK by-election, Liberal politician **David Steel** is first elected to Parliament, for the constituency of Roxburgh, Selkirk and Peebles.

Soviet cosmonaut Aleksei A Leonov is the first person to make a **space walk**, from *Voshkod 2*.

Gemini 3 is the first spacecraft to carry two people together into orbit. It is part of the US space programme.

US dramatist Neil Simon's comedy *The Odd Couple* opens in New York.

Motown's most successful female vocal group, the Supremes, have their fourth consecutive US number one with **'Stop! In the Name of Love'**.

English guitar hero **Eric Clapton** leaves the Yardbirds because the group has become 'too commercial'; he is replaced by Jeff Beck. Clapton goes on to join John Mayall's Bluesbreakers.

US marines invade the **Dominican Republic** to prevent an allegedly imminent communist takeover; the rebels claim to wish to return to the 1963 constitution of exiled former president Juan

Bosch. 40,000 US troops land at the request of the ruling junta, but the rebels hold out for four months in the city of Santo Domingo, despite thousands of casualties.

India and Pakistan at war over **Kashmir** (April–July and Sept).

Australia and New Zealand announce (April and May) that they are sending troops to **Vietnam** to aid the US forces.

The world's first commercial satellite is launched: *Early Bird* relays television programmes and telephone signals between Europe and North America.

The **UK borrows £500 million** from the International Monetary Fund.

US sculptor **David Smith** dies in a car crash at 59.

The British leg of **Bob Dylan's European tour** is recorded by US filmmaker D A Pennebaker for the documentary *Don't Look Back*.

First of all, God is a woman. Well, you take it from there.
US singer and songwriter **Bob Dylan**

The Beatles' main US challengers, the Byrds, have their first hit with Dylan's **'Mr Tambourine Man'**.

I looked into his eyes for a long time, and he was doing something in there!
David Crosby of the Byrds on his meeting with Bob Dylan

Liverpool United soccer team wins the FA Cup for the first time.

Algerian president **Ahmed Ben Bella** is overthrown by Col Houari Boumédienne and imprisoned.

Japan establishes diplomatic relations with **South Korea**.

Parliament votes to introduce a **corporation tax** in the UK.

English dramatist Harold Pinter's play *The Homecoming* opens in London. Vivien Merchant plays the female lead.

Motown Records release **'The Tracks of My Tears'** by Smokey Robinson and the Miracles.

The Maldives (islands in the N Indian Ocean) become independent from Britain, outside the Commonwealth, as a sultanate.

50,000 US troops arrive in **Vietnam**.

Alec Douglas-Home resigns as leader of the British Conservative Party, to give the party a more modern image, and is succeeded by Edward Heath.

I think it would be fair to say that he [Edward Heath] is no politician and certainly no Leader of the Opposition. He is essentially an able civil servant, but the Tories have no one better.
Newspaper proprietor **Cecil King** on the change in Conservative Party leadership

---

The **death penalty** is abolished (except for treason) in the UK. A Conservative amendment requires the measure to be confirmed 1969.

London telephone numbers begin the adaptation to **international direct dialling**: the local exchange code will be given in figures instead of letters from now on.

The Rolling Stones' song **'(I Can't Get No) Satisfaction'** becomes their first US number one.

US vocal duo **Sonny and Cher** have their first hit, 'I Got You, Babe'; Cher will become better known as an actress.

Bob Dylan outrages part of the Newport Folk Festival audience by performing with an electric band.

> *I am unable to see in Dylan anything other than a youth of mediocre talent. Only a completely noncritical audience nourished on the watery pap of pop music could have fallen for such tenth-rate drivel.*
> British folk singer **Ewan MacColl**

The Beatles' film *Help!* opens.

Voting Rights Act passed in the USA ends all attempts to restrict black people's right to vote.

Race riots in Watts, Los Angeles: 34 people are killed and 7,000 arrested, and the damage is estimated at $40 million.

In Athens, 10,000 people demonstrate against the Greek king, **Constantine II**.

Cigarette advertising is banned from British television.

Swiss Modernist architect and town planner **Le Corbusier** dies at 77. His last work is the Le Corbusier Centre, Zurich, Switzerland (built 1965–68).

Bob Dylan releases his classic rock album *Highway 61 Revisited*.

Singapore secedes from the Federation of Malaysia to become an independent republic within the Commonwealth, with Lee Kuan Yew as prime minister.

The UK Trades Union Congress accepts a statutory **prices and incomes policy**.

Natural gas is found under the North Sea and will eventually be supplied to British homes.

England gets its **first female high-court judge**, Elizabeth Lane.

UK car manufacturer **Aston Martin** introduces its first four-seater, the DB-6.

French theologian and organist **Albert Schweitzer**, Nobel Peace Prize winner, dies at 90.

After a coup attempt, the **Indonesian army massacres** between 200,000 and 700,000 people as suspected communists, acting in part on information given by the US Central Intelligence Agency. Hundreds of thousands are arrested without trial, left-wing parties and organizations are banned, and all political activity at local level is banned.

Britain refuses **Rhodesia's** demand for immediate independence because prime minister Ian Smith will not allow black participation in the government.

Mass demonstrations are held in the USA against the **Vietnam War** (from Oct).

A new US **immigration act** abolishes the national-origins quotas.

US poet **Randall Jarrell** dies at 51. In addition to poetry he wrote criticism, a campus novel, and children's books.

The term **'flower power'** is coined by US poet Allen Ginsberg.

The **Beatles** are created members of the Order of the British Empire for services to exports.

Rhodesia, S central Africa, makes a unilateral declaration of independence from Britain (11 Nov). The United Nations Security Council calls for sanctions.

Coup in the **Congo** (Zaire) makes Mobutu Sese Seko president.

The **New York blackout** (9 Nov): total power failure for about 12 hours in all of New York City as well as most of seven states and parts of Canada, affecting 30 million people.

A UK **motorway speed limit** of 70 mph is introduced.

The **Post Office Tower** is completed. At 304 m/1,000 ft, it is the tallest building in London, and has a revolving restaurant on top.

The musical *Man of La Mancha*, based on the novel *Don Quixote* by Spanish novelist Miguel de Cervantes Saavedra (1547–1616), opens in New York and will run for 2,329 performances.

English rock group the Who release '**My Generation**', their trademark hit.

> *I smash guitars because I like them. I usually smash a guitar when it's at its best.*
> English rock musician **Pete Townshend** of the Who

US promoter Bill Graham puts on his first rock concert at the **Fillmore Auditorium**, San Francisco, which will become a focal point of the hippie movement. On the bill are the Grateful Dead and Jefferson Airplane.

Jean-Bédel Bokassa seizes power in the **Central African Republic** in a military coup.

The first **space rendezvous** is carried out by US spacecraft *Gemini* 6 and 7: they manoeuvre very close but do not dock.

A US Navy Skyhawk jet bomber falls off the deck of the ship *Ticonderoga* 130 km/80 mi off the coast of Japan, sinking with its load of a one-megaton hydrogen bomb.

The musical *Charlie Girl* opens in London and will run for 2,202 performances; among the cast is Anna Neagle.

The play *Cactus Flower* by Abe Burrows opens in New York to run for 1,234 performance.

'**Day Tripper**' / '**We Can Work It Out**' by the Beatles is the Christmas charttopper in the UK.

US vocal group the Mamas and the Papas release their classic first record, **'California Dreamin''**.

US duo Simon and Garfunkel's **'Sounds of Silence'** is released as a single, to top the US chart by Jan 1966.

Liu Shaoqi, China's state president from 1960, is deposed.

China enters the **Vietnam War** on the side of North Vietnam.

Ferdinand Marcos is elected president of the Philippines.

Suleyman Demirel becomes prime minister of Turkey.

World food aid peaks 1965–66 at 167 million tonnes.

Phosphate deposits are discovered in Western Sahara, which re-kindles Moroccan interest in this disputed territory.

Tibet becomes an 'autonomous region' of China, but the original boundaries are not respected.

US president **Johnson** shows reporters his scars from a gall-bladder operation.

The **Confederation of British Industry (CBI)**, an employers' organization, is formed by merger of the Federation of British Industries, the British Employers' Confederation, and the National Association of British Manufacturers.

The **Greater London Council** is established, a single local authority for the capital.

British police officers on the beat are issued with **two-way radios**.

UK **Rent Act** reintroduces rent controls and tenant security previously abolished by the Conservative government.

UK **Race Relations Act** bans discrimination in public places and sets up the Race Relations Board.

London Zoo's **golden eagle** escapes twice this year, cheered on by the public.

Poor harvests in overcropped Kazakhstan forces the USSR to buy wheat from Canada and Australia, though not from the USA, because of its condition that half the shipments be made in US vessels.

Exceptionally severe **drought in India and Pakistan** causes famine.

A reduced fish catch off the coast of Peru is attributed to **El Niño**, a periodic warm current; a 200-fold increase in fishing by Peru 1945–62 may also be a factor. Stocks of sardine-type fish have suddenly halved to an est. 12 million tonnes.

Commercial whalers slaughter 20,000 **sei whales**, the peak catch for the species, other whales having become scarce or out of bounds.

Insulin is the first protein to be synthesized.

The concept of **plate tectonics** is formulated by Canadian geophysicist J Tuzo Wilson.

Fossil bacteria are found by US palaeontologist Elso Sterremberg Barghoorn in rock 3.5 bn years old – the first known microfossils.

Europe's longest bridge is opened, the **Zeeland Bridge** in the Netherlands.

The **Betamax videotape** recording system is introduced by Sony.

Stereo LP records are on the market.

Soft contact lenses are developed.

The first **scanning electron microscope** goes on sale, produced by the Cambridge Instrument Company, UK.

The psychedelic drug **LSD** (lysergic acid diethylamide) is banned in the USA (1966 in the UK).

US car manufacturers are forced to add safety features after the publication of Ralph Nader's *Unsafe at Any Speed*.

Tobacco companies in US are forced to add a **health warning** to US cigarette packets.

The first **supercomputer**, the US Control Data CD6600, is introduced. A supercomputer performs basic operations in picoseconds (thousand-billionths of a second) rather than nanoseconds (billionths of a second).

Microwave ovens are developed in Japan.

The **Routemaster** double-decker bus is designed for London Transport by Douglas Scott.

Japanese car manufacturers **Honda** win their first Formula One Grand Prix, in Mexico City.

Kingsley Hall, E London, opens as an **antipsychiatry commune** led by avant-garde psychiatrists R D Laing and David Cooper.

The **universities of Kent and Warwick** are founded in England.

The **Free University of New York** opens, the first of several to be attempted in the climate of student rebellion.

The *Sun* newspaper begins publication in the UK, as a broadsheet.

The War Game, a drama documentary about nuclear war made for the BBC by Peter Watkins, is banned by senior officials for giving an unfavourable picture.

Till Death Us Do Part, a BBC comedy series satirizing intolerance and ignorance, begins.

The US television series *The Fugitive*, starring David Janssen, wins the Emmy award for Best Drama Series.

British actress **Diana Rigg** takes over the female lead in the television series *The Avengers*.

The **Salk Institute for Biological Studies** is built in La Jolla, California, designed by Estonian-born US architect Louis Kahn.

English Op-art painter **Bridget Riley** wins the Venice Biennale prize.

German artist Joseph Beuys creates the performance piece *24 Hours*, in which he stands on a white box for that length of time, performing various movements and actions with surrounding objects.

Anglo-US poet, dramatist, and critic **T S Eliot** dies; born 1888. His highly influential works include *The Waste Land* 1922 and *Murder in the Cathedral* 1935.

Japanese novelist **Jun'ichirō Tanizaki** dies; born 1886. His main work is *The Makioka Sisters* 1943–48.

English novelist Margaret Drabble publishes *The Millstone*.

US science-fiction writer Frank Herbert publishes the first book of his *Dune* series.

International Festival of Poetry at the Royal Albert Hall, London, draws 7,000 people to hear the US Beat poets and the Liverpool performance poets; this is the first emergence of the British underground, or counterculture.

English novelist John Fowles publishes the mystifying *The Magus*.

Scottish novelist Muriel Spark publishes *The Mandelbaum Gate*.

US director Richard Lester's British-made film *The Knack* stars Rita Tushingham.

French actresses Brigitte Bardot and Jeanne Moreau star in Louis Malle's film *Viva Maria*.

US film comedy *What's New, Pussycat?* stars Peter Sellers, Peter O'Toole, and Woody Allen.

Indian producer **Ismail Merchant** and US director **James Ivory** make their first film together, *Shakespeare Wallah*.

Italian film director Federico Fellini makes the Surrealist *Giulietta degli spiriti/Juliet of the Spirits*, starring Giulietta Massini.

French film director Jean-Luc Godard makes *Alphaville* and, in colour, *Pierrot le fou*.

British actor Terence Stamp stars in the film *The Collector*.

Belgian film director Agnes Varda makes the idyllic tragedy *Le Bonheur*.

English director David Lean's film of Boris Pasternak's novel *Dr Zhivago* stars Julie Christie and Omar Sharif.

The film *Darling* by English director John Schlesinger stars Julie Christie and Dirk Bogarde.

English dramatist Edward Bond creates controversy with his play *Saved*, in which a baby is stoned to death.

The Killing of Sister George by British dramatist Frank Marcus has its premiere at Bristol Old Vic; transferred to London, the play will run for a year.

German theatre company the **Berliner Ensemble**, guesting at the Old Vic, London, perform several of Bertolt Brecht's works, including *Die Dreigroschenoper/The Threepenny Opera*, for which Kurt Weill wrote the music.

English stage director **Trevor Nunn** joins the Royal Shakespeare Company, where he will direct a number of classic plays over the next few years.

English actress Maggie Smith plays the title role in August Strindberg's *Miss Julie* at the Old Vic Theatre, London.

English ballet dancer Margot Fonteyn and her Russian partner Rudolf Nureyev create the title roles in Kenneth McMillan's ballet *Romeo and Juliet* at the Royal Opera House, Covent Garden, London.

US choreographer **Twyla Tharp** produces her first work.

Hungarian-born Austrian composer György Ligeti writes the piece *Requiem*.

US opera singer **Maria Callas** gives her last public performance, in *Tosca*, at the Royal Opera House, Covent Garden, London.

US composer Arnold Schoenberg's opera *Moses und Aron*, written 1932–51, has its premiere at the Royal Opera House, Covent Garden, London.

The year's best-selling country-and-western record is US singer and songwriter Roger Miller's **'King of the Road'**.

Welsh pop singer Tom Jones has his first hit, **'It's Not Unusual'**.

Singer and actor **Charles Aznavour** is the highest-paid French entertainer.

The **International Society for Krishna Consciousness** is founded in New York. Its followers, with shaved heads and orange robes, will soon spread to other Western cities, chanting 'Hare Krishna'.

US religious leader Jim Jones establishes the **Peoples Temple** cult in N California.

French fashion designer **André Courrèges** launches his Space Age collection.

The **miniskirt** appears in Britain.

US photographer **Richard Avedon** joins *Vogue*; he will become the highest-paid fashion and advertising photographer in the world.

1966

After the second General Election within two years, Harold Wilson's Labour government was returned to power with a substantial majority. The result did nothing to help the economy which, throughout the year, despite pay and price freezes, continued to deteriorate. In the summer of 1966, Britain responded to the economic gloom with an outpouring of patriotic fervour. For England hosted and won the soccer World Cup. England's winning captain Bobby Moore and the England manager Alf Ramsay became heroes of the hour. Britain's economy might have lost the 'feel-good' factor, but the public felt great about this England's finest sporting hour. Meanwhile, the situation in South Vietnam continued to worsen as hundreds of thousands of American troops poured into that land. In the United States and Europe, the first signs of political dissent at US foreign policy began to appear.

On the death of India's prime minister **Lal Bahadur Shastri** at 61, **Indira Gandhi** comes to power.

Military **coup in Nigeria** led by Ibo officers causes resentment among other ethnic groups.

Military **coup in Upper Volta** (Burkina Faso) removes President Maurice Yaméogo and installs Col Sangoulé Lamizana. He dissolves the national assembly and bans all political activity (until 1969).

Australian prime minister **Robert Menzies** retires, and is succeeded by Harold Holt, also of the Liberal Party.

A **B-52 bomber** of the US Air Force collides with the tanker plane when refuelling in midair; both planes crash. The B-52 is carrying four hydrogen bombs. Two are recovered intact, after a long search; the other two break up and scatter plutonium over the Palomares village in Almería province, Spain.

Swiss sculptor **Alberto Giacometti** dies at 64.

English novelist **Evelyn Waugh** dies; born 1903. His works include *Decline and Fall* and *Viles Bodies*.

> *He died of snobbery.*
> English photographer **Cecil Beaton** on the death of novelist Evelyn Waugh at 62

The musical *Sweet Charity*, based on a Federico Fellini film, opens on Broadway in New York.

Coup in Uganda by prime minister Milton Obote deposes the king-cum-president Sir Edward Mutesa II.

Ghana's president **Kwame Nkrumah** is deposed by a military coup while on a visit to China.

Soviet writers **Andrei Sinyavsky** and **Yuri Daniel** are sentenced to labour camps at the start of a clampdown on dissidents. Both had had their novels smuggled to the West for publication.

Soviet spacecraft *Luna 9* makes the first soft landing on the Moon.

A charter airline, **Laker Airways**, is launched by British entrepreneur Freddie Laker.

US silent-film comedian **Buster Keaton** dies at 70.

Indonesian general **Raden Suharto** assumes power as emergency ruler.

General election in the UK. Both Labour and Conservative parties include in their manifestos a promise to build 0.5 million new houses. Labour increases its parliamentary majority to 96.

> *The electorate haven't had enough time to see our actions put into effect and recognize them as failures.*
> British Labour politician **Richard Crossman** on his party's victory in the March general election

Soviet space probe *Venera 3* crashes on Venus, the first human-made object to reach another planet.

US illustrator **Maxfield Parrish** dies at 95.

Pope Paul VI meets archbishop of Canterbury Michael Ramsey: it is the first official meeting of the heads of the two churches for 400 years.

The **Moors Murders trial** starts at the Old Bailey, London; Ian Brady and Myra Hindley will get life sentences for killing five or more children, whom they buried on the Pennine moors near Manchester in N England.

Space probe *Luna 10* goes into orbit around the Moon, another first for the Soviet space programme.

The Rolling Stones release *Aftermath*, their first album of all original material.

British Guiana, South America, achieves independence, within the Commonwealth, as Guyana.

A **strike by the National Union of Seamen** begins in the UK (16 May–2 July).

The musical *Mame* by Jerry Herman opens in New York and will run for more than 1,500 performances. It stars Angela Lansbury.

Bob Dylan tours the UK with the Band; his Royal Albert Hall concert, London, will be widely bootlegged.

US vocal group the Mamas and the Papas have their second big hit, **'Monday, Monday'**.

The Rolling Stones release **'Paint It Black'**, another number one, the first rock record to feature a sitar.

Military **coup in Argentina** ends 11 years of civilian rule.

US airborne forces bomb the main cities of **North Vietnam**, Hanoi and Haiphong, for the first time.

Large **civil-rights demonstrations** in the US South; race riots in Cleveland, Ohio (June–July).

US Moon probe *Surveyor 1* makes a soft landing on the Moon and sends back photographs.

The first **credit card** in the UK (Barclaycard) is launched.

French sculptor **Hans Arp** dies at 78.

'**River Deep – Mountain High**' by Ike and Tina Turner is a UK hit but its comparative failure in the USA drives its producer Phil Spector into retirement.

US tennis player **Billie Jean King** wins the women's singles at Wimbledon for the first time.

A second military **coup in Nigeria** puts Col Yakubu Gowon in power. Tens of thousands of Ibos are massacred.

France withdraws from the military integration of **NATO**, though not from the alliance.

Malawi becomes a one-party (right-wing) republic, with the Malawi Congress Party the only permitted political organization.

Thailand and the Philippines send troops to assist the USA in the **Vietnam War**.

US airborne forces bomb the demilitarized zone of **Vietnam** for the first time.

France moves its **nuclear-bomb testing** from N Africa to the South Pacific. Between now and 1974, France will conduct atmospheric tests from the uninhabited atolls of Mururoa and Fangataufa in French Polynesia.

President **Mobutu** of the Congo (Zaire) replaces the colonial names of the country's cities: Léopoldville becomes Kinshasa, Elisabethville Lubumbashi, and Stanleyville Kisangani.

Race riots in the cities of Chicago and Atlanta, USA.

Black is beautiful.
Slogan of US Black Power movement

A **wage freeze** is introduced in the UK.

Gwynfor Evans takes his seat in Parliament, the first **Welsh Nationalist** to do so.

Bob Dylan is seriously injured in a motorcycle accident, and the album *Blonde on Blonde* is his last for two years.

The trio **Cream** is formed in London, with Ginger Baker (drums), Jack Bruce (guitar), and Eric Clapton (guitar). The band's unusual time signatures and extended improvisations will accelerate the development of heavy rock and art rock.

England wins the **soccer World Cup** for the first time, by defeating Germany. The team is captained by Bobby Moore and England's football manager is Alf Ramsay – both become heroes of the hour.

The **Cultural Revolution** begins in China (until 1969). Artists and academics are persecuted by student Red Guards.

Indonesia and **Malaysia** reach a peace agreement, the former ceasing to attempt to undermine the latter.

Premiere in Austria of German composer Hans Werner Henze's opera *The Bassarids*.

US comedian **Lenny Bruce** dies of an overdose at 39. His jokes challenged taboos concerning sex, religion, and racism.

English sailor **Francis Chichester** sets out in his boat *Gypsy Moth IV* on a solitary circumnavigation of the world.

The Beatles' *Revolver* album is notable for Indian influence and tape-loop experiments.

An unexpected symbol of our trust in the future and of our longing for a place for us all to live in.
Mario Savio of the US Free Speech Movement, decoding the Beatles' song 'Yellow Submarine'

Bechuanaland, in central southern Africa, achieves independence from Britain, within the Commonwealth, as Botswana. Seretse Khama is the country's first president.

Henrik Verwoerd, South African prime minister and chief promoter of apartheid, is assassinated in parliament. His successor is Balthazar Vorster.

South Africa's mandate over **South West Africa** (now Namibia) is terminated by the United Nations (UN), but South Africa ignores this and extends its apartheid laws to the territory, generating armed resistance.

Cameroon becomes a one-party state when its political parties are merged into the Cameroon National Union.

The UK's first **nuclear submarine** is launched.

The Times is acquired by Canadian media magnate Lord Thomson of Fleet, who already owns the *Sunday Times*. The classified advertisements are taken off the front page of *The Times*.

The first episodes of the US science-fiction television series *Star Trek* are broadcast.

US dramatist Edward Albee's play *A Delicate Balance* opens in New York.

The opera *Antony and Cleopatra* by US composer Samuel

Barber opens the new Metropolitan Opera House in Lincoln Center, New York.

US television creates a mop-topped pop group, the **Monkees**, for a weekly series of the same name; it is broadcast in the UK from Jan 1967. The four actors are immediately criticized for not playing on their first record, 'Last Train to Clarksville'.

Basutoland, S Africa, achieves independence from Britain, within the Commonwealth, as the kingdom of Lesotho. Chief Leabua Jonathan is the first prime minister.

The British army officially ceases **racial discrimination**.

Convicted British spy **George Blake** escapes from prison and flees to the East bloc.

A slag heap collapsing in **Aberfan**, Wales, buries a school and houses and kills 144 people.

UK car manufacturer **Jensen** launches its Interceptor model.

International Times, Europe's first underground paper, is launched in London; after an enforced name change to *IT*, it will grow to have a circulation of 50,000 by 1968.

San Francisco rock band **Jefferson Airplane** find a new singer: model Grace Slick.

Barbados, island country in the Caribbean, achieves independence from Britain, within the Commonwealth. Errol Barrow is the country's first prime minister.

Heavy storms cause **flooding in N Italy**: two-thirds of Florence is under water, with enormous damage to buildings and works of art. The clean-up will take years.

US Republican politician **Ronald Reagan** is elected governor of California, taking office Jan 1967.

*No, no! Jimmy Stewart for governor, Reagan for best
friend.*
US film producer **Jack Warner**, of Warner Bros, when told
that Ronald Reagan was a candidate for governor of
California

The BBC television play *Cathy, Come Home*, written by Jeremy
Sandford (broadcast Nov), dramatizes the problem of homeless-
ness and leads to the foundation of the charity Shelter.

The introduction of **post codes** begins in the UK.

The musical *Cabaret* , set in Berlin and based on a story by
Christopher Isherwood, opens in New York.

The **Jimi Hendrix Experience**, having played one gig in Paris,
make their London debut. The rock trio becomes instantly famous
for Hendrix's innovative guitar work.

US former surf group the Beach Boys' **'Good Vibrations'** is the
most expensive single yet produced, and a huge hit (Nov–Dec).

British prime minister Harold Wilson and Rhodesian prime minister Ian Smith meet on board HMS *Tiger* in the Mediterranean,
but fail to agree. Smith declares **Rhodesia** a republic. Mandatory
sanctions imposed by the UN are ignored by South Africa and
Portugal.

The **San Francisco Diggers**, a radical, wishful group, celebrate
'the death of money'.

The last *Ready Steady Go!* programme is broadcast in the UK
with the Who as the last guests.

Walt Disney, creator of the US cartoon-film empire, dies.

The **UFO club** opens in London and becomes a weekly meeting
place for the underground.

In the **Dominican Republic**, Joaquín Balaguer, a former member of deposed dictator Rafael Trujillo's cabinet, returns from exile and is elected president. Suppressing dissent, he has political opponents killed; some 2,000 are made to 'disappear'.

King Mwambutsa IV of **Burundi**, after a 50-year reign, is deposed by one of his sons, who in turn is deposed by prime minister Michel Micombero, and Burundi becomes a republic.

Social Democrat **Willy Brandt**, mayor of West Berlin from 1957, becomes foreign minister of West Germany.

Famine continues in **India**.

Drought begins in the **Sahel** area of Africa, and will continue into the following decades, contributing to famine.

Senegal becomes a one-party state when the only legal opposition party is incorporated in the Senegalese Progressive Union (UPS).

The settlement on **South Georgia** in the S Atlantic is abandoned, but the island remains a British crown colony.

Burmese nationalist **U Nu** is exiled.

Angolan right-wing nationalist movement **UNITA** is founded by Jonas Savimbi, with South African backing; it is the Portuguese colony's third independence movement.

The **National Organization of Women** is launched in the USA by feminist writer Betty Friedan.

The **Black Panther Party** is founded in the USA by Huey Newton and Bobby Seale.

Juliet Mitchell's article 'Women: The Longest Revolution', published in *New Left Review*, sparks the **feminist movement** in the UK.

The UK's first **student sit-in** takes place at the London School of

Economics; over the next two years demands spread for more democratic participation by students everywhere.

The first **Notting Hill Carnival** is held in London.

The US space agency NASA completes its **Gemini programme**, in which astronauts practise space walks and docking of spacecraft.

The first two probes of the US **Lunar Orbiter** series are launched (Aug and Nov) to photograph the Moon in preparation for the Apollo landings.

Oil is discovered beneath the **North Sea**. Exploitation of this resource will transform Norway's economy.

A **tidal power station** opens in the gulf of St Malo, Brittany, France.

A **nuclear-fuel reprocessing plant** opens at Cap de la Hague on the coast of Normandy, France.

Sizewell A nuclear power station, Suffolk, England, comes into operation with a Magnox reactor.

The fast reactor at the **Enrico Fermi nuclear plant** near Detroit, Michigan, suffers partial meltdown of the core, threatening to contaminate the whole city.

In the **Antarctic**, specially protected areas are established internationally for animals and plants.

A variety of **rice**, IR-8, that gives a particularly high yield is developed at the International Rice Research Institute in the Philippines. It requires heavy fertilization and will prove vulnerable to blight.

California introduces legislation to limit **air pollution** from motor vehicles, effective from 1969 and affecting only new models.

Measles vaccine is introduced.

The immobilization of **enzymes** is achieved.

Laser radar, which can pinpoint small targets, is developed in Japan.

The idea of using **optical fibres** for telecommunications is first proposed in the UK.

Dolby Laboratories in the USA develop the **Dolby noise-reduction system**.

Disposable nappies are test marketed in the USA.

The comic-book-style television show *Batman* begins (until 1968).

The puppet television programme *Thunderbirds* begins.

British dramatist John Hopkins writes *Talking to a Stranger*, four plays for BBC Television.

Cambridge University history faculty, by British architect James Stirling, is completed.

German-born US Abstract Expressionist painter **Hans Hofmann** dies; born 1880.

The Velvet Underground avant-garde rock group collaborate on **multimedia shows** with Pop artist Andy Warhol in New York. This is also the year Warhol exhibits *Clouds*, silver pillows floating in the air.

John Lennon meets Japanese artist **Yoko Ono** at an exhibition of her work in London. They become inseparable.

French artist Niki de Saint-Phalle, known for her colourful sculptures of outsize female figures, creates the largest one yet at the Moderna Museet in Stockholm, Sweden: *Hon/She* lies on her back and spectators can enter through a doorway between her legs and walk around in her. The figure is subsequently destroyed.

French philosopher Michel Foucault publishes *Les Mots et les choses/The Order of Things*.

> *As an archaeology of our thought easily shows, man is an invention of recent date. And one perhaps nearing its end.*
> French philosopher **Michel Foucault**, *The Order of Things*

US writer Truman Capote publishes *In Cold Blood*, which he describes as a 'nonfiction novel'; it documents a multiple murder.

English novelist Paul Scott publishes the first volume of his Raj Quartet, *The Jewel in the Crown*.

US writer John Barth publishes the novel *Giles Goat-Boy*.

Irish poet Seamus Heaney publishes *Death of a Naturalist*.

English novelist Graham Greene sets his *The Comedians* in Haiti.

Austrian ethologist Konrad Lorenz publishes *On Aggression*.

US writer and critic Susan Sontag publishes *Against Interpretation*, a collection of essays that includes the influential **'Notes on Camp'** 1964.

Italian writer Italo Calvino publishes *Le cosmicomiche/Cosmicomics*, experimental stories.

Nigerian novelist Chinua Achebe publishes *A Man of the People*.

English children's writer William Mayne publishes the novel *Earthfasts*.

Italian director Michelangelo Antonioni depicts 'swinging London' in his film *Blow-Up*, starring David Hemmings and Vanessa Redgrave.

Karel Reisz makes the film *Morgan: A Suitable Case for Treatment* with Vanessa Redgrave and David Warner.

English film actor Michael Caine stars in *Alfie*, directed by Lewis Gilbert.

Spanish Surrealist Luis Buñuel makes the film *Belle de Jour*, starring Catherine Deneuve.

Swedish director Ingmar Bergman makes the film *Persona*, starring Bibi Anderson and Liv Ullman.

French director François Truffaut films Ray Bradbury's novel *Fahrenheit 451* around the housing estates of Roehampton, London.

Jiri Menzel's *Ostre sledované vlaky/Closely Observed Trains* is the most successful Czechoslovak film of the decade.

The romantic film *Un homme et une femme/A Man and a Woman* by French director Claude Lelouch stars Anouk Aimée and Jean-Louis Trintignant.

Polish director Roman Polanski's film *Cul de Sac* stars English actor Donald Pleasence and French actress Françoise Dorléac.

French film director Robert Bresson releases *Au Hasard Balthazar*.

Edward Albee's play *Who's Afraid of Virginia Woolf?* is filmed by Mike Nichols with Elizabeth Taylor and Richard Burton.

French film director Alain Resnais's *La Guerre est finie* has a screenplay by Jorge Semprun; it stars Yves Montand and Ingrid Thulin.

Italian director Gillo Pontecorvo makes the political film *La battaglia di Algeri/The Battle of Algiers*.

US actor James Coburn stars in *Our Man Flint*, the first of a series of James Bond spoof films.

English dramatist Joe Orton's black comedy *Loot* opens in London.

Polish director Jerzy Grotowski's **Theatre Laboratory** tours outside Poland for the first time, in Scandinavia. Their experimental techniques will influence Western theatre.

English actor David Warner plays **Hamlet** in London.

In London, Peter Brook stages *US* with the Royal Shakespeare Company, a collective theatre production (no author) about the Vietnam War.

English dramatist Christopher Hampton makes his debut with ***When Did You Last See My Mother?*** at the Royal Court Theatre, London, where he becomes resident playwright on the strength of its success.

Belcher's Luck by English dramatist David Mercer is given its premiere by the Royal Shakespeare Company in London.

English actress Margaret Rutherford plays Mrs Malaprop in Richard Sheridan's *The Rivals*.

The **School of Contemporary Dance** is founded in the UK; the London Contemporary Dance Theatre grows from this.

English choreographer Anthony Tudor creates *Shadowplay* for the Royal Ballet.

US jazz pianist Keith Jarrett joins the **Charles Lloyd Quartet**, popular for a time with both jazz and rock audiences.

Novelty hit **'Winchester Cathedral'** by the studio-created New Vaudeville Band was 1966's best-selling British record in the USA.

English teenager **Twiggy** becomes a supermodel.

Paper dresses are the year's most ephemeral fashion.

English soccer player **Bobby Charlton** is European Footballer of the Year.

Belgian cyclist **Eddie Merckx** wins his first classic race, Milan to San Remo.

1967

This was a year of wars and of serious economic and political disappointments. The Six-day Arab–Israeli War highlighted the world's failure to resolve the Middle East crisis. The war resulted in an overwhelming Israeli victory, the occupation by Israel of the lands of many Arab states, and the bitter resentment of the dispossessed Palestinian peoples. In Vietnam, the war escalated out of control, despite massive US troop commitments and large-scale aerial bombardment of the North. Many people in Europe and America reacted to this escalation by actions of mass protest and, in 1967, the first major anti-Vietnam rallies were seen on the streets of Britain. British pride took a number of serious knocks in 1967. First, there was what was then the worst-ever incident of pollution, when the oil tanker *Torrey Canyon* ran aground and succeeded in polluting many of Britain's West Country beaches. More significantly, in November 1967, the government was forced to devalue the pound sterling.

Israel uses tanks in its border conflict with Syria.

Three US Apollo astronauts become the first casualties of the space programme when they are killed in a **fire at Cape Kennedy** (Cape Canaveral).

Soviet nuclear-powered icebreaker *Lenin* is abandoned in the Arctic after suffering a **reactor meltdown**.

In England, the new town of **Milton Keynes** is founded.

The first **'human be-in'**, or hippie gathering, draws 20,000 people in Golden Gate Park, San Francisco. Media coverage of this event precipitates a mass migration by young people to the Haight-Ashbury district of San Francisco.

Donald Campbell, British holder of the world land- and water-speed records, is killed in the Lake District, NW England, when trying to break the latter.

General **Raden Suharto** replaces Achmed Sukarno as president of Indonesia.

The British *Boy's Own* magazine folds.

Persistent efforts by the drug squad in Britain lead to the **arrests of Mick Jagger, Keith Richards, their girlfriends, and associates** (Feb and after). A judicial attempt to make an example of them causes an outcry.

I've never had problems with drugs, only policemen.
English rock guitarist **Keith Richards**, of the Rolling Stones

---

The Beatles' **'Strawberry Fields Forever'** / **'Penny Lane'** is their first single since 1962 not to reach number one in the UK chart.

The Beatles release their ground-breaking album *Sergeant Pepper's Lonely Hearts Club Band*, with an album cover from Pop artist Peter Blake.

US psychedelic rock group Jefferson Airplane release *Surrealistic Pillow.*

The army takes control in **Sierra Leone**: two coups in rapid succession follow the refusal of the ruling party to accept electoral defeat.

The worst ever oil spill in British waters is caused by the tanker *Torrey Canyon* running aground off Cornwall.

Helicopters are used by police in the UK for the first time.

The suspension of two student leaders at the London School of Economics triggers a **sit-in**.

A rumour spreads from Berkeley, California, that it is possible to get high by **smoking banana peel**.

The **Stax Soul Revue** tours the UK. Performers include Otis Redding, Sam and Dave, and Booker T and the MGs.

The first **Velvet Underground** album, with the Andy Warhol-designed banana sleeve, is released (March USA, Oct UK).

US folk-rock group Buffalo Springfield warn against police brutality in **'For What It's Worth'**. Band members include Neil Young.

Military **coup in Greece**; the king is deposed and all political activity banned. The junta, known as 'the colonels', will last until 1974.

In New York, 400,000 people demonstrate against the **Vietnam War.**

Soviet cosmonaut **Vladimir Komarov** is killed when his craft *Soyuz I* crash-lands on Earth.

The US pavilion at Expo '67 in Montréal, Canada, is one of Buckminster Fuller's **geodesic domes**.

Czech-born British dramatist Tom Stoppard's play *Rosencrantz and Guildenstern Are Dead* is produced at the Old Vic Theatre, London. (A shorter version was given at the Edinburgh Festival Fringe in 1966.)

Forty-one bands play, often simultaneously, at the 14-Hour **Technicolor Dream** hippie event at Alexandra Palace, N London, attended by 10,000.

English pop singer Sandie Shaw wins the *Eurovision Song Contest* with **'Puppet on a String'**. It was inane material like this that prompted her early retirement, she later admitted.

The state of **Biafra** declares independence from Nigeria and civil war breaks out (it will cost 1 million lives before it ends with Biafra's reabsorption).

French president Charles de Gaulle vetoes a second British application to join the **European Economic Community** (EEC).

Breathalyzer tests for motorists are introduced in the UK.

A Magnox nuclear reactor in Annan, Scotland, undergoes a partial meltdown. The **Chapelcross** plant was built to produce plutonium for nuclear weapons. The reactor has to be shut down for more than a year.

US painter **Edward Hopper** dies at 84. His cityscapes and interiors are strongly atmospheric and melancholy.

A Day in the Death of Joe Egg by English dramatist Peter Nichols opens at the Citizens' Theatre, Glasgow.

Quadrophonic sound is first used in concert, by psychedelic rock band Pink Floyd in their *Games for May* at the Queen Elizabeth Hall, London.

Jimi Hendrix's electric guitar playing on the LP *Are You Experienced* extends the vocabulary of the instrument.

US protest rock group Country Joe and the Fish release the psychedelic album *Electric Music for the Mind and Body*.

Liverpool's Roman Catholic **cathedral** opens.

The **Arab–Israeli Six-Day War** (5–10 June) results in Israeli expansion: the Gaza Strip is occupied for the second time, and Israel seizes the Sinai peninsula, the Golan Heights, the West Bank of the River Jordan, and the Arab part of Jerusalem. The Suez Canal is blocked by Egypt; in the next few years this will lead to the construction of supertankers that would not fit through it anyway. Many Palestinian refugees settle in Lebanon.

If we lose this war, I'll start another in my wife's name.
Israeli minister of defence **Moshe Dayan** on the Six-Day War

China explodes its first **hydrogen bomb**.

The first **cash-dispensing machine** in the UK is introduced by Barclays Bank.

Dorothy Parker, US writer and wit, dies at 73; she will be remembered for her sardonic poems and short stories.

English children's writer and journalist **Arthur Ransome** dies at 83; he wrote the Swallows and Amazons series of novels.

The Beatles record **'All You Need Is Love'** watched by a worldwide television audience of 400 million.

At the **Monterey Pop Festival** in California, performers include Jimi Hendrix, the Who, the Grateful Dead, and Otis Redding. The event is filmed by D A Pennebaker as *Monterey Pop*.

Visiting Canada, French president **de Gaulle** shouts '*Vive le Québec libre*/Long live free Québec!', which does not go down well with the Canadian government.

The USA sees **race riots** in 127 cities, the worst being in Detroit, Michigan, and Newark, New Jersey (June–Aug). Federal troops are called out to suppress the Detroit riots, in which 43 people are killed, more than 2,000 injured, and 5,000 become homeless after fires.

South African politician **Albert Luthuli** dies; born 1899. He was president of the African National Congress.

The UK **Sexual Offences Act** legalizes homosexual acts in private between consenting adults, but the age of consent is higher than for heterosexuals.

A full-page advertisement in *The Times* (24 July) advocating the **legalization of cannabis** is signed by a number of well-known people, including Nobel prizewinner Bernard Crick, novelist Graham Greene, and painter Richard Hamilton.

The organization **Release** is founded in London to help people who have been arrested for drug possession.

BBC television begins transmitting in colour; all major US networks are transmitting entirely in colour by this date.

News at Ten begins on the ITV channel in the UK.

German dramatist Rolf Hochhuth's semidocumentary play *Soldaten/Soldiers*, dealing with World War II, opens in West Berlin.

US jazz saxophonist **John Coltrane** dies at 40; he was one of the most influential figures in jazz.

US psychedelic rock band the Doors break through with **'Light My Fire'**, a US number one.

US folk singer Arlo Guthrie becomes an overnight success at the Newport Folk Festival, Rhode Island, with his 18-minute monologue **'Alice's Restaurant'**.

The USA admits to having carried out continual aerial bombardment of **Laos** for the past three years.

The first **pulsar** (celestial source that emits pulses of energy) is discovered by British astronomers Jocelyn Bell and Antony Hewish.

The **Dartford Tunnel** under the River Thames in E London is opened.

Britain's offshore **pirate radio stations** are closed down.

A three-day rock festival, or **'love-in'**, is held in the grounds of Woburn Abbey, England.

Fleetwood Mac play their first gig; at this time they are a British blues band.

Referendum in **Gibraltar** gives a majority for remaining in association with the UK.

BBC radio is reorganized into Radio One, Two, Three, and Four.

Sweden changes to driving on the right.

The transatlantic liner *QE2* is launched by the Queen.

US avant-garde blues band Captain Beefheart and the Magic Band release their first album, *Safe as Milk*.

Whimsical Scottish folk group the Incredible String Band release *5,000 Spirits, or The Layers of the Onion*, bringing psychedelia to the folk scene and vice versa.

US folk singer and songwriter **Woody Guthrie** dies at 52. His song 'This Land Is Your Land' has become an alternative US national anthem.

Argentine-born revolutionary leader **Che Guevara** is killed in Bolivia.

The **Abortion Law Reform Act** puts an end to back-street abortions in the UK; the **Dangerous Drugs Act** also becomes law.

The first of many demonstrations is held outside the US embassy in London against the **Vietnam War** and against the British government's support of US participation in it. In Washington DC, 100,000 protesters attempt to levitate the Pentagon (Defense Department headquarters) by chanting.

They've got to stop their aggression, or we're going to bomb them back into the Stone Age.
US general **Curtis LeMay** on his policy for North Vietnam

A symbolic funeral of 'Hippie, son of Media' is held in San Francisco, marking the end of the **Summer of Love**.

The rock musical *Hair*, by Galt MacDermot and Ragni and James Rado, opens off-Broadway in New York. It will transfer to Broadway and run for some 1,800 performances.

Scottish pop singer Lulu stars with US actor Sidney Poitier in the film *To Sir with Love*.

Sterling is devalued by 14.3% (18 Nov), giving a US exchange rate of $2.40.

---

*It does not mean, of course, that the pound here in Britain
in your pocket or purse or in your bank has been devalued.*
UK prime minister **Harold Wilson** announcing devaluation

Morning sittings are introduced at the House of Commons, but the experiment proves unpopular with those MPs who have other jobs, and is soon abandoned.

The office of parliamentary **ombudsman** is introduced in the UK, to deal with complaints about the work of civil servants.

Nuclear submarine **HMS *Repulse*** is launched at Barrow-in-Furness, Lancashire, and promptly runs aground.

Radio Leicester, the UK's first **local radio** station, begins broadcasting.

Rolling Stone magazine begins publication in San Francisco. It will keep to its mixture of rock and politics but grow less radical with commercial success.

South African surgeon Christiaan Barnard performs the first human **heart-transplant** operation. The patient lives for another 18 days.

The **electronic quartz watch** is introduced by Swiss watchmakers.

The Beatles' experimental film *Magical Mystery Tour* is premiered on BBC 1; it is generally regarded as disappointing.

The **First Czechoslovak National Festival of Rock Music** is held in Prague, where the counterculture soon turns sharply political.

Police raiding the California laboratory of legendary underground chemist Augustus Owsley Stanley III find enough **LSD** for 750,000 doses.

US soul singer **Otis Redding** is killed in a plane crash in Wisconsin at 26.

US psychedelic rock group Love release their finest work, *Forever Changes*.

The **People's Republic of South Yemen**, in SW Asia, is formed by the union of Aden and the Federation of South Arabia when they achieve independence from Britain.

As part of its policy of **Africanization**, Kenya puts pressure on its residents from former British colonies in Asia to leave the country.

Antigua and **Barbuda**, islands in the E Caribbean, become an associated state within the Commonwealth, with internal independence.

St Christopher, **Nevis**, and **Anguilla** (islands in the E Caribbean) achieve internal self-government, within the Commonwealth.

A **coup in Togo** puts Etienne Gnassingbé Eyadéma in power.

Brussels, Belgium, becomes the seat of the EEC.

Fruit and vegetables are destroyed to keep prices high under the **Common Agricultural Policy** of the EEC.

Croatian nationalist **Franjo Tudjman** is expelled from the League of Communists of Yugoslavia.

After a referendum in Australia, full citizenship rights are extended to **Aborigines**.

Alexander Dubček becomes first secretary of the Communist Party in Czechoslovakia.

With continued famine, **India** imports 6 million tonnes of wheat from the USA.

White supremacist **Lester G Maddox** becomes governor of Georgia, USA.

US radical activist **Abbie Hoffman** disrupts the New York stock exchange by dropping dollar bills to the trading floor.

Death of British Labour politician **Clement Attlee** who, as prime minister 1945–51, presided over the introduction of the welfare state; born 1883.

The **steel industry** is nationalized in the UK as the British Steel Corporation.

British MP **Jo Grimond** resigns from the Liberal Party leadership and is succeeded by **Jeremy Thorpe**.

Jennie Lee becomes Britain's first minister for the arts.

The **Northern Ireland Civil Rights Association** is set up to press for equal treatment for Roman Catholics and Protestants in the provinces.

The **National Front** fascist party is founded in the UK.

US Black Power leader **Stokely Carmichael** addresses the Dialectics of Liberation conference in London, calling for 'counter-violence' and sabotage against the state.

Trinidad-born black nationalist **Michael X** becomes the first person to be prosecuted under the UK Race Relations Act, for allegedly inflammatory remarks.

Element 105, **hahnium**, is first produced in the USA.

Italian carmakers **Fiat** overtake Volkswagen in motor-vehicle production.

The **Krasnoyarsk Dam** in Siberia, on the Yenisei River, is built, with the world's largest hydroelectric power station.

The Soviet series of **Venus** probes continues and establishes the composition of the planet's atmosphere, which is the hottest in the Solar System owing to the greenhouse effect.

British biologist John B Gurden is the first to **clone** a vertebrate animal – a frog.

The drug **L-dopa** is found successful in treating Parkinson's-disease sufferers.

Contraception becomes legal in France.

US tobacco company Philip Morris launches the **Virginia Slims advertising campaign** with the slogan 'You've come a long way, baby'; the subsequent increase in smoking among teenage girls has nothing to do with it, Philip Morris will insist.

The UK abandons **nuclear testing** at the Maralinga site in the South Australian desert and launches a clean-up. An est. 23 kg/50 lb of plutonium will remain on the site.

LP sales surpass sales of singles in the USA, where over $1 billion is spent this year on records.

Cassette tapes come on the market at a UK price of 40 shillings, or £17.94 at 1993 prices.

Television series *The Prisoner* is first shown in the UK. This mysterious science-fiction story, created by and starring Patrick McGoohan, acquires a cult following in later years.

I am not a number – I am a free man!
  Catch phrase in British television series *The Prisoner*

The **beanbag chair** is introduced.

Three Italian designers come up with a transparent, inflatable **PVC armchair, Blow**.

The **O-Series of scissors** designed by Olof Bäckström 1960 goes into production at Fiskars, Finland. The kitchen scissors become a classic.

US television programme *Rowan and Martin's Laugh-In* begins.

> *Sock it to me!*
> Catch phrase in US television series *Rowan and Martin's Laugh-In*

Australian magazine *Oz* begins publication in London; it is the world's only underground magazine in full colour.

John Galsworthy's novel series *The Forsyte Saga* is televised in the UK, starring Eric Porter.

UK television series *Callan* begins.

Television puppet show *Captain Scarlet* begins.

The **John Hancock Center** in Chicago, Illinois, is built, one of the world's tallest skyscrapers.

The **Yamanashi Press Centre**, Konju, Japan, by Kenzō Tange, is an example of Metabolist architecture, which can be expanded.

Belgian Surrealist painter **René Magritte** dies.

Broken Obelisk by US artist Barnett Newman is a sculpture of geometric shapes.

A British bookseller is convicted under the **Obscene Publications Act** for selling Hubert Selby Jr's novel *Last Exit to Brooklyn*.

Nigerian writer **Wole Soyinka** is imprisoned (until 1969).

Colombian novelist Gabriel García Márquez publishes the magic-realist *Cien años de soledad/One Hundred Years of Solitude*.

British novelist V S Naipaul publishes *The Mimic Men*.

Indian novelist R K Narayan publishes *The Vendor of Sweets*.

English magic-realist writer Angela Carter publishes the novel *The Magic Toyshop*.

English novelist A S Byatt publishes *The Game*.

Czech writer Milan Kundera's first novel, *The Joke*, brings him into official disfavour.

English novelist Angus Wilson publishes *No Laughing Matter*.

English poet Ted Hughes publishes *Wodwo*.

Britain's poet laureate **John Masefield** dies; he was born 1878.

A Grain of Wheat by Kenyan novelist Ngugi wa Thiong'o describes exploitation of the people by the post-independence government.

The book on human behaviour, *The Naked Ape* by Desmond Morris, curator of mammals at London Zoo, becomes a best-seller.

US novelist Alison Lurie publishes *Imaginary Friends* about a sociologist and a group of UFO cultists.

English writer A L Barker publishes the novel *The Middling*.

English writer Alan Garner publishes the haunting teenage novel *The Owl Service*.

English writer Leon Garfield publishes the Dickensian children's novel *Smith*.

Flambards is the first of a historical novel trilogy for children by British writer K M Peyton.

Expatriate US director Joseph Losey makes the film *Accident* from a script by Harold Pinter, starring Dirk Bogarde and Stanley Baker.

US actress Jane Fonda stars in the light-hearted science-fiction film *Barbarella*.

Swedish director Bo Widerberg's film *Elvira Madigan* is a romantic tragedy.

US actor Dustin Hoffman makes his name in Mike Nichols's film *The Graduate*.

English director John Schlesinger films Thomas Hardy's novel *Far from the Madding Crowd* with Julie Christie, Alan Bates, Terence Stamp, and Peter Finch.

Warren Beatty and Faye Dunaway star in US director Arthur Penn's film *Bonnie and Clyde*.

French film director Robert Bresson makes *Mouchette*.

Italian film director Pier Paolo Pasolini makes *Oedipus Rex*.

US actors Rod Steiger and Sidney Poitier star in the film *In the Heat of the Night*, directed by Norman Jewison.

English dramatist **Joe Orton** is killed by his lover, who then commits suicide.

English actor Roy Dotrice creates a one-person show, *Brief Lives*, based on the life and work of English 17th-century biographer and antiquary John Aubrey. It opens at the Hampstead Theatre Club and will transfer first to Broadway, New York, and in 1969 to the West End, London.

English actor Alec McCowen stars in *Hadrian VII* by Peter Luke, based on the writings of Frederick Rolfe, at the Birmingham Repertory Theatre and later in London and New York.

British dramatist Simon Gray's *Wise Child* opens in London, starring Alec Guinness.

English actress **Vivien Leigh** dies; she was born in India 1913. Her roles include Scarlett O'Hara in *Gone With the Wind* 1939, Blanche du Bois in Tennessee Williams's *A Streetcar Named Desire* (stage 1949, film 1951), and Cleopatra in Shakespeare's *Antony and Cleopatra* with Laurence Olivier 1951.

Russian dancer **Mikhail Baryshnikov** joins the Kirov Ballet in Leningrad (St Petersburg), USSR.

US composer Aaron Copland writes *Inscape for Orchestra*.

US composer Elliott Carter writes *Symphony for Three Orchestras*.

The opera *Arden Must Die* by British composer Alexander Goehr is given its premiere by the Hamburg Staatsoper.

US jazz guitarist **Larry Coryell** and vibraphone player **Gary Burton** join forces.

US composer Frank Zappa releases two satirical albums this year with his band the Mothers of Invention, *Absolutely Free* and *We're Only in It for the Money*.

US country singer Bobbie Gentry has a number-one hit with her first record, **'Ode to Billy Joe'**; its mysterious narrative becomes the basis for a film 1976.

US country singer Merle Haggard releases his classic songs **'Sing Me Back Home'** and **'I'm a Lonesome Fugitive'**.

US soul singer Aretha Franklin has a series of US number-one hits, including **'Respect'**.

The American football **Super Bowl** match is first held.

The World Boxing Association takes away the heavyweight title from **Muhammad Ali** because of his refusal to be drafted into the US Army.

No Vietcong ever called me nigger.
US boxer **Muhammad Ali** on refusing to be drafted into the army

---

Welsh rugby union player **Gareth Edwards** is appointed captain of his country at 20.

1968

In 1968, the world saw a ray of hope in the Prague Spring, when Dubček's communist Czechoslovakian state attempted to liberalize itself, only to be crushed later in the year by Soviet-led troops. This was the year of the Tet Offensive, when the North Vietnamese Army overran the South, and demonstrated to the world that it could not be defeated by the United States. In the United States, Martin Luther King, the civil rights campaigner was gunned down, as was Bobby Kennedy, younger brother to the late president, while campaigning for the presidency. That prize went to Richard Nixon. In Europe there were marches and civil disorder. Despite dire warnings, there was little trouble in mainland Britain. Instead, to the amazement of many, the ancient troubles in Ireland erupted, as calls for civil rights in the British-ruled province of Northern Ireland turned into serious rioting. So, in the United Kingdom, the year of drugs, rock and roll, and protest ended with bloodshed, and the beginning of a new chapter in the troubled history of Britain in Ireland.

The South Pacific island of **Nauru** achieves independence from Australia, New Zealand, and the UK, with 'special member' Commonwealth status.

Spy ship **USS *Pueblo*** is captured by North Korea; its crew is released at the end of the year.

The USA loses its 10,000th aircraft over **Vietnam**.

Tet Offensive in Vietnam (Jan–Feb): prolonged attack by Vietcong on some 30 towns in South Vietnam, including Saigon.

Liberal **John Gorton** becomes prime minister of Australia on the death of Harold Holt.

A US Air Force **B-52** bomber carrying nuclear weapons crashes near Thule air base, Greenland. An area of 25 sq km/9.6 sq mi is contaminated with radioactive material, and the clean-up takes until Sept. This is the tenth accident in 11 years involving a bomber carrying nuclear arms, and US secretary of defence Robert McNamara orders nuclear weapons to be removed from planes on airborne alert.

English director **Trevor Nunn** succeeds Peter Hall as head of the Royal Shakespeare Company.

The musical *Promises, Promises*, by US songwriting team Burt Bacharach and Hal David, opens in New York; it will run for 1,281 performances.

US rock group the Velvet Underground's album *White Light/White Heat* is released (Jan USA, May UK).

Kenya expels its Asian population; those with British passports begin to arrive in the UK.

A US domestic flight is hijacked and forced to land in Cuba. Copy-cat **hijackings** follow, and searches of passengers and luggage are gradually instituted at airports worldwide.

UK **Immigration Act** restricts entry to those who can claim a British-born grandparent.

Transcendental meditation, as taught by Maharishi Mahesh Yogi, attracts Western celebrities to India, including the Beatles.

Mauritius, island in the Indian Ocean, achieves independence from Britain, within the Commonwealth. Its first prime minister is Seewoosagur Ramgoolam.

Massacre of 109 Vietnamese civilians in the village of **My Lai**, South Vietnam, by US troops.

US Federal Bureau of Information director J Edgar Hoover promulgates his secret **Counter-Intelligence Program** against black nationalist groups. The tactics include *agents provocateurs* and misinformation.

The musical *Canterbury Tales* opens in London, to run for more than 2,000 performances. The music is by Richard Hill and John Hawkins and the lyrics by Noell Coghill.

US civil-rights leader **Martin Luther King Jr** is assassinated in Memphis, Tennessee (4 April). Riots break out in more than 40 cities, resulting in 46 deaths and 21,270 arrests.

I may not get there with you, but I want you to know
tonight that we as a people will get to the promised land.
US civil-rights leader **Martin Luther King**, speech on the eve of his assassination

Czechoslovak Communist Party leader Alexander Dubček launches a campaign of liberalization, with the aim of creating 'socialism with a human face', which becomes known as the **Prague Spring**.

Liberal politician **Pierre Trudeau** becomes prime minister of Canada.

German student leader **Rudi Dutschke** is shot; riots ensue.

A French trawler in the Irish Sea finds a US **Polaris submarine** caught in its nets. This will become fairly commonplace.

Conservative politician Enoch Powell warns of **'rivers of blood'** unless immigrants are repatriated from the UK (20 April); for this speech in Birmingham he loses his shadow-cabinet post.

Like the Roman, I seem to see the River Tiber foaming with
much blood.
British Conservative politician **Enoch Powell**, speaking against immigration

Gay play *The Boys in the Band* is the debut of US dramatist Mart Crowley. It will run for 1,000 performances in New York and be a success in London 1969.

US dramatist Arthur Kopit's play *Indians* has its world premiere in London, staged by the Royal Shakespeare Company at the Aldwych Theatre.

'Mrs Robinson' by Simon and Garfunkel is taken from the sound-track of *The Graduate*.

Scottish-born motor-racing driver **Jim Clark** is killed during a Formula Two race at Hockenheim, West Germany.

The French students' and workers' uprising known as the **'May events'** begins (3 May) in Paris when student protesters at the Sorbonne University take over the Latin Quarter. Days of street fighting culminate in a general strike.

The first **liver** and the first **lung transplants** are carried out in the UK; the lung patient dies within a fortnight.

US country singer Johnny Cash's live album *At Folsom Prison* is released and will spend 122 weeks in the US charts.

Welsh singer **Mary Hopkin** is discovered by model Twiggy and signed up by the Beatles' Apple record company.

US Democrat politician **Robert Kennedy** is assassinated (5 June) while campaigning for the presidential nomination in California.

French president **Charles de Gaulle** is forced by continued pro-test demonstrations to call elections, which he wins.

US Pop artist **Andy Warhol** is shot by an extremist feminist and seriously injured (3 June).

Elvis Presley performs in front of a live audience for the first time since 1961, recording a Christmas television special (not shown in the UK until 31 Dec 1969).

The first of a series of **free concerts in London's Hyde Park** features Pink Floyd, Jethro Tull, and other rock groups.

The **Nuclear Nonproliferation Treaty** is signed by 36 countries.

The last customs barriers go down in the **European Community**.

General **William C Westmoreland** becomes US Army Chief of Staff.

British Labour politician **David Owen**, who entered Parliament 1966, is made undersecretary for the Navy. He will defect to form the Social Democratic Party.

The **Hayward Gallery** on London's South Bank is officially opened.

US heavy-rock group Iron Butterfly have their biggest success with *In-a-Gadda-Da-Vida*.

US hard-rock band Steppenwolf have a US number two with **'Born to Be Wild'**.

Papal encyclical *Humanae Vitae* reaffirms the Roman Catholic Church's opposition to contraception.

Two-hundred thousand Warsaw Pact troops invade **Czechoslovakia** on Soviet orders (20–21 Aug) to restore the orthodox communist line. Dubček is arrested. In the face of popular resistance, more than 400,000 additional troops are sent in.

France tests its first **hydrogen bomb** in the South Pacific.

The **Democratic Party convention** in Chicago, Illinois, attracts about 10,000 demonstrators, who are outnumbered and clubbed by rioting police.

The **Sadler's Wells Opera** company moves into the Coliseum Theatre, London.

US-Canadian group the Band, who have been backing Bob Dylan, release their first album *Music from Big Pink*.

The first **Isle of Wight rock festival**, S England, draws 8,000 people.

Swaziland, SE Africa, achieves independence from Britain, within the Commonwealth, under King Sobhuza II.

Military **coup in the Congo**: Marien Ngouabi overthrows Alphonse Massamba-Débat and dissolves the country's only legal party.

The Philippines advances a territorial claim on **Sabah**, a state of Malaysia on NE Borneo.

The **Victoria Line** of the London Underground is opened, running from Highbury to Walthamstow; it will be extended to Victoria 1969.

Post within the UK is divided into first and second class.

Television police series *Hawaii Five-O*, starring Jack Lord, begins in the USA.

Theatre **censorship** is abolished in the UK.

US musical *Hair* opens in London.

US blues band Big Brother and the Holding Company release their second album, *Cheap Thrills*; their vocalist Janis Joplin leaves for a solo career.

US tennis player **Arthur Ashe** wins the US Open.

Equatorial Guinea, W central Africa, achieves independence from Spain. The country's first president, Francisco Macias Nguema, soon assumes dictatorial powers.

President Lyndon B Johnson announces that US bombardment of **Vietnam** N of the 20th parallel will cease (31 Oct). Peace talks fail, however, because the South Vietnamese junta refuses to participate if the National Liberation Front is present.

Civil-rights demonstrators are attacked and 100 injured in Londonderry (Derry), Northern Ireland (5 Oct): start of the **Troubles**.

Student rebellion in Mexico City ends with gunfire by police and federal troops; many demonstrators are killed.

French-born US artist **Marcel Duchamp** dies at 81, having retired from painting decades earlier to play chess. He was one of the founders of the Dada movement.

The first **MC5** album is recorded live in Detroit, Michigan, where the band are part of the radical political scene.

Presidential election in the USA is won by Republican **Richard M Nixon**. His Democrat opponent was Vice President Hubert Humphrey, Lyndon Johnson having refused to run for re-election.

US anti-war demonstrators burn their **draft cards** (Nov and later).

Black Panther leader **Eldridge Cleaver** goes into exile in Cuba.

You're either part of the solution or you're part of the problem.
US Black Panther leader **Eldridge Cleaver**

The Beatles' **White Album** is released.

Britain's longest student **sit-in**, at Bristol University, ends after 11 days with the start of the Christmas holidays.

The world's first **supersonic airliner**, the Russian TU-144, flies for the first time.

US Nobel prizewinning novelist **John Steinbeck** dies at 68. He was the author of *The Grapes of Wrath* 1939 and other realistic novels.

The Rolling Stones' album *Beggars Banquet*, produced by Jimmy Miller, is released.

Irish singer and songwriter Van Morrison releases the album *Astral Weeks*.

US pop singer Marvin Gaye has a US number one on Motown Records with **'I Heard It Through the Grapevine'**.

Japan adopts a defence policy that rules out nuclear weapons.

Hungary begins economic decentralization.

In Canada, the **Parti Québecois** is founded, advancing the interests of the French-speaking population.

Military **coup in Iraq**: Major-General Ahmed Hassan al-Bakr makes himself head of state and government.

Japan's **gross national product** overtakes that of West Germany.

A revolt in **Chad** by the increasingly active Frolinat guerrillas is quelled with military help from France.

France tests its first **thermonuclear bombs** in Polynesia at Fangataufa and Mururoa atolls; the former becomes too contaminated to set foot on for six years.

Britain begins to withdraw its forces from Bahrain, which joins two other British-held territories, Qatar and the Trucial States (the United Arab Emirates), to form the **Federation of Arab Emirates**.

The sultan of the **Maldives** is deposed and a republic declared.

Military **coup in Mali**: Moussa Traoré seizes power.

South West Africa is redesignated Namibia by the United Nations, but South Africa retains control by force.

Australian right-wing politician **Joh Bjelke-Petersen** becomes premier of Queensland.

Basque separatists in France and Spain begin a guerrilla campaign to secure a united Basque state.

Military **coup in Peru**, led by General Juan Velasco Alvarado. The Sendero Luminoso Maoist guerrillas become increasingly active.

Portugal's military dictator António de Oliveira Salazar is succeeded by **Marcello Caetano**.

In the continuing Nigerian civil war, there is famine in the breakaway state of **Biafra**, and thousands are dying.

Army revolt in **Sierra Leone**; Siaka Stevens becomes prime minister.

The West German urban guerrilla **Baader-Meinhof** gang (Red Army Faction) begin direct action in Europe against what they perceive as US imperialism.

US labour leader **Cesar Chavez** calls for a boycott of California grapes.

A **plague of locusts** destroys crops in Saudi Arabia and NE Africa.

The tanker *World Glory* spills more than 51 million litres of oil off South Africa.

Testing **nerve gas** in Utah, the US Army accidentally kills thousands of sheep.

Unpopular measures to rein in the UK's finances include the introduction of **prescription charges** and an end to the provision of **free school milk** in secondary schools.

The UK decides to stay on **British Summer Time** throughout the year. The experiment is discontinued 1970.

In the UK, the Wootton Commission recommends the decriminalization of **cannabis** use; its proposals are rejected by the government.

UK **Race Relations Act** is extended to housing and employment.

The UK **Foreign Office** and **Commonwealth Office** are merged.

The **British Leyland** company is formed by merger of British Motor Holdings and Leyland Motors.

The UK **Ministry of Health** is reorganized as the Department of Health and Social Security, under Richard Crossman.

Further **demonstrations** are held outside the US embassy in London – 25,000 people in March, 50,000 in Oct – and are violently suppressed by police.

Part of the **Ronan Point** tower block in London collapses as a result of a gas explosion.

Squatting becomes, in the UK and elsewhere, a semilegal way of using empty property and a high-profile movement for communal self-help.

The **Wankel engine** is first used in some German and Japanese cars.

Intercontinental ballistic missiles are equipped with **multiple warheads** that can be directed to individual targets.

Exploitation of **Alaska's oil reserves** begins.

LP sales surpass sales of singles in the UK.

Eight-track tape cartridges are marketed. This format is killed off the following year.

Electroweak interaction is discovered by particle physicists Steven Weinberg and Sheldon Lee (USA) and Abdus Salam (Pakistan). It combines what was previously thought to be two separate particle interactions, the weak and the electromagnetic.

The science of **astrochemistry** takes off with the discovery of molecules of three or more atoms (such as water, ammonia) in interstellar space.

Pulsars are recognized to be rotating neutron stars, very small and dense and spinning very fast.

Brain hormones are discovered by Roger Guillemin and Andrew Schally.

Pollution is estimated to kill 15 million fish a year in the USA alone.

The *Doonesbury* political comic strip is created by 19-year-old Garry Trudeau in the USA, becoming syndicated 1969.

British architect Denys Lasdun's buildings for the **University of East Anglia** at Norwich are completed.

Italian abstract artist **Lucio Fontana** dies; born 1899.

Japanese sculptor Tomio Miki creates a series of *Ears* cast in aluminium.

English art critic **Herbert Read** dies; born 1893. His work includes *The True Voice of Feeling* 1953.

C Day Lewis is appointed Britain's poet laureate.

English novelist Iris Murdoch publishes *The Nice and the Good*.

US writer Norman Mailer publishes *The Armies of the Night*, about the 1967 peace march to the Pentagon.

Soviet writer Alexander Solzhenitsyn has two documentary novels published abroad, *Rakovy korpus/Cancer Ward* and *V kruge pyervom/The First Circle*.

US writer Gore Vidal publishes the novel *Myra Breckinridge*.

French-based academic Christine Brooke-Rose writes the experimental novel *Between* without using the verb 'to be'.

English biographer Michael Holroyd publishes the second volume of his life of **Lytton Strachey** (the first came out 1967).

English science-fiction writer Keith Roberts publishes the novel *Pavane*, set in an alternative Britain where the Reformation never took place.

Open the pod door, Hal.
US science-fiction writer **Arthur C Clarke**, script for film *2001: A Space Odyssey*

US-born British film director Stanley Kubrick makes *2001: A Space Odyssey*.

British director Lindsay Anderson makes the film *If ...* about a public-school rebellion.

Polish director Roman Polanski, working in the USA, makes the horror film *Rosemary's Baby*.

French film director François Truffaut makes *Baisers volés/Stolen Kisses*.

Italian director Pier Paolo Pasolini's film *Teorema* stars Terence Stamp in a mute role.

French film director Claude Chabrol makes *Les Biches/The Girlfriends*.

English comedian **Tony Hancock** commits suicide; born 1924.

English actress Julie Christie stars in Richard Lester's film *Petulia*.

Italian director Franco Zeffirelli films Shakespeare's *Romeo and Juliet*.

Barbra Streisand repeats her Broadway role in William Wyler's film of the musical *Funny Girl*.

French director Jacques Rivette makes the film *L'Amour fou*.

The US film *Yellow Submarine* features animated cartoon versions of the Beatles and has some original music by them.

Zero Mostel and Gene Wilder star in the film *The Producers* directed by US comedian Mel Brooks.

If you've got it, flaunt it.
US comedian **Mel Brooks** in film *The Producers*

French political thriller *Z*, directed by Costa-Gavras, stars Yves Montand and Jean-Louis Trintignant.

Hollywood science-fiction film *Planet of the Apes*, with Charlton Heston, will have many sequels and spawn a television series.

English dramatist Alan Bennett's play *Forty Years On* opens, starring John Gielgud.

English dramatist Edward Bond's play *Narrow Road to the Deep North* opens.

US dancer **Gelsey Kirkland** joins the New York City Ballet, where she soon becomes a star.

Arthur Mitchell, the first black principal dancer to join the New York City Ballet, founds the **Dance Theatre of Harlem**.

English choreographer Frederick Ashton creates the ballet *Enigma Variations*.

The opera *Taverner* by English composer Peter Maxwell Davies is completed.

English composer Andrew Lloyd Webber and lyricist Tim Rice write their first musical, *Joseph and the Amazing Technicolor Dreamcoat*.

The musical *Cabaret* opens in London with Judi Dench in the leading role; it had its premiere in New York 1966.

US country singer Jeannie C Riley gets to number one with her first record, **'Harper Valley PTA'**.

US country singer Tammy Wynette writes, with her producer Billy Sherrill, the song with which she will always be identified, **'Stand by Your Man'**.

Songs of Leonard Cohen is a commercial and critical success for the Canadian poet, songwriter, and singer.

Swiss Protestant theologian **Karl Barth** dies.

French couturier **Pierre Cardin** is the first women's designer to show a collection for men.

Jacqueline Kennedy, widow of the murdered US president, marries Greek shipping tycoon Aristotle Onassis.

US athletes Tommy Smith and John Carlos give **Black Power salutes** at the Mexico Olympics.

British equestrian **Richard Meade** wins three gold medals in the Olympic Games.

Czechoslovak gymnast **Vera Caslavska** wins four gold medals in the Olympic Games.

US swimmer **Mark Spitz** wins four Olympic gold medals.

Italian motorcyclist **Giacomo Agostini** wins the junior and senior Isle of Man TT races and the 350-cc world title, all on MV Agusta.

Irish soccer player **George Best** is European Footballer of the Year.

English motor-racing driver **Graham Hill** becomes Formula 1 world champion for the second time, for Lotus.

West Indian test cricketer **Gary Sobers** scores six 6s in an over, a world record.

The Wimbledon tennis championship is won by Australian **Rod Laver** (men's singles) and American **Billie Jean King** (women's singles).

1969

This was the year the United States harnessed its economic power to science and technology, and put the first astronauts on the Moon. It was also the year Richard Nixon took over the United States presidency, and immediately and secretly began to extend the Vietnam War into neutral Cambodia. In Britain, the troubles in Northern Ireland turned into pogroms. The British Army was sent to Belfast and Londonderry to protect Irish Catholics from attack by their Protestant neighbours. As Britain recovered from the economic ravages of the mid-1960s, visible signs of prosperity were evident as more people (despite currency restrictions) began to take overseas package holidays; Spain proved to be a particularly popular destination. In addition, the spread in motor cars, telephones, and home ownership reached postwar highs.

Richard Nixon is inaugurated as US president.

You can say that this Administration will have the first complete, far-reaching attack on the problem of hunger in history. Use all the rhetoric, so long as it doesn't cost money.
US president **Richard Nixon**, official minutes of White House meeting

---

Czechoslovak student **Jan Palach**, 21, sets himself on fire in Wenceslas Square, Prague, in protest against the Soviet military presence. His death makes him a national hero, and others follow his example.

British employment minister Barbara Castle's White Paper *In Place of Strife* is published. This forms the basis of an Industrial Relations Bill, which is eventually withdrawn after pressure from trade-union leaders.

Learie Constantine becomes the UK's first black life peer.

Switzerland's first, experimental nuclear reactor undergoes **partial meltdown**. The cave in which it was built is sealed off to become a nuclear-waste repository.

The **Boeing 747 jumbo jet** is test-flown.

Australian media magnate Rupert Murdoch acquires control of UK Sunday newspaper the *News of the World*.

The **Beatles** make their last public performance, on the roof of the Apple Corps offices in London, recording 'Get Back' (30 Jan).

Death of Indian mystic **Meher Baba**, who had not spoken for 43 years. He was the guru of several British rock musicians.

Yassir Arafat becomes president of the Palestine Liberation Organization (PLO).

The **first test-tube fertilization** is carried out at Cambridge University.

English art historian Kenneth Clark makes the television series *Civilization*, broadcast on BBC 2 (Feb–May).

Opera, next to Gothic architecture, is one of the strangest inventions of Western man. It could not have been foreseen by any logical process.
British art historian **Kenneth Clark**, *Civilization*

US bombing raids on communist bases in neutral **Cambodia** begin.

Labour politician **Golda Meir** becomes prime minister of Israel.

Anguilla declares itself a republic, separate from its association with St Christopher-Nevis; British troops meet little resistance in suppressing the rebellion.

Anglo-French **Concorde** supersonic airliner makes its first test flight.

The third, self-titled **Velvet Underground** LP is released (March USA, April UK).

The **Kray brothers**, E London gangsters, are tried at the Old Bailey. Ronald and Reginald Kray are convicted of murder and Charles Kray as an accessory.

Slovak politician **Gustav Husák** replaces Alexander Dubček as leader of the Communist Party in Czechoslovakia.

French president **Charles de Gaulle** resigns after a referendum defeat. His successor (elected June) is former prime minister **Georges Pompidou**.

Student leader **Daniel Cohn-Bendit** is deported from France to West Germany.

Nous sommes tous des juifs allemands./*We are all German Jews.*
French student slogan when revolutionary leader Daniel Cohn-Bendit was described as a German Jew by the authorities

---

In a UK by-election, Irish independent republican **Bernadette Devlin** is elected to Parliament for the Mid-Ulster constituency at the age of 21.

The Who release the double album *Tommy*, later to become a film and a stage show.

There are strikes and mass demonstrations in **Curaçao**, Netherlands Antilles, against a wage freeze and rising unemployment. It prompts some economic reform and is the beginning of a nationalist movement among the poor of the island.

135   *Vietnam*

John Lennon and Yoko Ono record **'Give Peace a Chance'** in their hotel bedroom in Montréal, Canada.

Spain closes the border with **Gibraltar**.

Border clashes between **China** and the **USSR** (June–Aug) on the Ussuri River in E Asia, and in Central Asia.

The **'soccer war'** between El Salvador and Honduras (June–July): border conflict coincides with football match.

President Nixon announces the start of US troop withdrawal from **Vietnam**.

Millions of fish die in the **River Rhine**; an accidental leak of insecticide is identified as the cause.

New York police raid the Stonewall, a gay bar in Greenwich Village, and the patrons fight back (29 June). This incident is seen as the start of the **Gay Liberation Front**.

US film actress and cabaret singer **Judy Garland** dies at 47; she starred in many film musicals, including *The Wizard of Oz* 1939.

The first LP by vocal supergroup **Crosby, Stills & Nash** (released June) will spend 100 weeks in the US chart.

US astronauts **Neil Armstrong** and **Edwin Buzz Aldrin** of *Apollo 11* become the first people to walk on the Moon (20 July).

The death of a woman in a car belonging to US senator Edward Kennedy at **Chappaquiddick**, Massachusetts, in circumstances never fully explained, scuppers his chances of the presidency.

Prince Charles is invested as Prince of Wales.

German architect **Walter Gropius** dies at 86. He was a founder of the influential Bauhaus school of architecture and design 1919.

The Rolling Stones play a **free concert in Hyde Park**, London, for some 250,000 people, two days after the death of founder member Brian Jones at 24.

English pop singer and songwriter David Bowie releases **'Space Oddity'**, his first hit.

Military junta takes power in **Brazil** on the resignation of the incumbent president.

Return to civilian government in **Ghana**; elections won by Kofi Busia.

Londonderry in Northern Ireland is proclaimed **'free Derry'** amid sectarian riots. British troops are sent in.

US space probes *Mariner 6* and *7* send back pictures of the equator and southern hemisphere of Mars.

German architect **Ludwig Mies van der Rohe** dies at 83; he was director of the Bauhaus school 1929–33 and worked in the USA from 1937. The National Gallery, Berlin 1963–67, is among his last works.

Woodstock, the first free rock festival, is held in New York State (15–17 Aug); 400,000 people see the Who, the Band, Jefferson Airplane, Jimi Hendrix, and others. A documentary film is made of the event.

The second **Isle of Wight**, S England, rock festival features Bob Dylan.

Members of the **Charles Manson** 'family' murder five people in Beverly Hills, California. Celebrity victims and elements of sex, drugs, and religious cult make this a big media case.

Libyan revolution: the king is deposed by Moamer al-Khaddhafi, making the country a one-party Islamic state.

North Vietnamese leader **Ho Chi Minh** dies at 79.

The **Chicago Eight trial** begins: US political activists including Tom Hayden, Bobby Seale, and Abbie Hoffman are accused of conspiring to cause a riot at the Democratic convention 1968. Seale, bound and gagged in the courtroom, is sentenced to four years for contempt of court.

Two-hundred-and-fifty squatters are evicted from **144 Piccadilly**, London, where they have generated much publicity for the housing crisis.

We are the writing on your wall.
Slogan of squatters at 144 Piccadilly, London

The Beatles' *Abbey Road* album is released. The cover picture starts the 'Paul is dead' rumour.

The **Plastic Ono Band**, including John Lennon and Eric Clapton, play their first concert at the Toronto Peace Festival, Canada.

The first **bootleg album** (with possible opera exceptions) appears. It is known as the *Great White Wonder* and contains unreleased material by Bob Dylan.

Army **coup in Somalia**: Mohamed Siad Barre comes to power.

Military **coup in Sudan** brings Mohammed Nimeri to power.

Socialist politician **Willy Brandt** becomes chancellor of West Germany.

Kenyan opposition leader **Oginga Odinga** is detained and his party banned; cabinet minister **Tom Mboya** is assassinated.

Conservative politician **Margaret Thatcher** becomes shadow education spokesperson.

US Beat Generation novelist **Jack Kerouac** dies of drink at 47 in Florida. His works include *On the Road* 1957 and *The Dharma Bums* 1958.

'I Want You Back' by US pop group the Jackson 5 marks the debut of ten-year-old **Michael Jackson** (Oct; Jan 1970 in UK).

The comedy programme *Monty Python's Flying Circus* begins on BBC television.

This parrot is no more. It's ceased to be. It's expired. It's gone to meet its maker. This is a late parrot. . . . It would be pushing up the daisies if you hadn't nailed it to the perch. . . It's an ex-parrot.
English comedian **John Cleese** in television programme *Monty Python's Flying Circus*

Hot Rats, a major work by US composer Frank Zappa, is released.

Mass demonstrations are held in the USA against the **Vietnam War**. President Nixon appeals to the 'silent majority' of Americans for support.

The great silent majority of my fellow Americans – I ask for your support.
US president **Richard Nixon**, television address on Vietnam War

---

A second **Moon landing** is carried out by two more US Apollo astronauts (14 Nov).

The children's educational television programme *Sesame Street* begins in the USA.

Work begins on building the **National Theatre** on the South Bank, London.

British blues-rock band **Cream** give their farewell concert at the Royal Albert Hall, London, later released as an album.

The all-white South African **Springbok** rugby team tours the UK despite anti-apartheid protests.

Agents of the US Federal Bureau of Investigation and police raid

Black Panther headquarters in Chicago, Illinois, and kill two of the party's leaders in their sleep. All others present are arrested, but the charges against them are eventually dropped.

Abolition of the **death penalty**, provisionally introduced 1965, becomes permanent in the UK after a vote in Parliament.

Friends underground news magazine begins publication in London; it will close, after name changes.

The Rolling Stones release *Let It Bleed*, and play a free concert at the Altamont Speedway in California. The Hell's Angels security guards kill a member of the audience.

James Chichester-Clark takes over from Terence O'Neill as prime minister of Northern Ireland.

Social Democrat **Olof Palme** becomes prime minister of Sweden.

Military **coup in Bolivia** follows President René Barrientos's death in a plane crash.

The first **Strategic Arms Limitation Talks (SALT)** begin in Helsinki, Finland, between US and Soviet leaders.

Anti-Chinese riots break out in **Kuala Lumpur**, Malaysia.

The **General Post Office** ceases to be a government department.

Wally Herbert of the British Transarctic Expedition makes the first surface crossing, by dog sled, of the Arctic Ocean (Alaska–Spitsbergen).

The **Internet** computer network is founded to transmit data between two military laboratories in the USA.

Measures to restrict the use of the insecticide **DDT** are introduced in Canada and parts of the USA.

Another first in Soviet space research: two **spacecraft dock** and cosmonauts transfer from one to the other.

Japanese geologists find nine **meteorites** in Antarctica – where they are easy to identify, lying on top of the ice sheet.

Ribonuclease is the first enzyme to be synthesized, by Chinese-born US biochemist Choh Hao Li.

The first **artificial heart** is used in a transplant operation in the USA. After three days it is replaced with a human heart.

The first **coronary bypass** operation is carried out. It involves replacing clogged coronary arteries (next to the heart) with blood vessels from another part of the patient's body. The procedure will become very common.

The food additive **monosodium glutamate** is found to cause brain damage in mice.

Danish designer Jakob Jensen's hi-fi **Beosystem 1200** for Bang & Olufsen has a Scandinavian state-of-the-art look.

The UK newspaper the *Sun* is bought by Australian entrepreneur Rupert Murdoch and its image is changed to increase circulation.

In the USA, the *Saturday Evening Post* ceases publication and *Penthouse* magazine is launched.

Redevelopment of **Les Halles** in Paris begins when the wholesale food market is moved to the outskirts of the city.

British sculptor **Anthony Caro** has a solo show at the Hayward Gallery, London.

Conceptual art makes its British debut with Gilbert and George presenting themselves as living sculpture.

British artist Barry Flanagan creates the work *Hole in the Sea*: sinking a cylinder into the beach, he films it as it is gradually submerged by the swirling tide.

US novelist Philip Roth publishes his best-selling, comic novel *Portnoy's Complaint*.

British writer Ronald Blythe publishes the social history *Akenfield: Portrait of an English Village*, whose oral-documentary approach will prove influential.

US writer Kurt Vonnegut Jr publishes the novel *Slaughterhouse-Five*, which draws on his World War II experience of the fire-bombing of Dresden, Germany.

US writer Russell Hoban settles in Britain and publishes the children's fantasy *The Mouse and His Child*.

US writer Ursula Le Guin publishes the science-fiction novel *The Left Hand of Darkness*.

English writer John Fowles publishes the historical novel *The French Lieutenant's Woman*.

The Four-Gated City is the last of British writer Doris Lessing's *Children of Violence* novel sequence, which began 1952 with *Martha Quest*.

French philosopher Michel Foucault publishes *L'Archéologie du savoir/The Archaeology of Knowledge*.

US engineer and architect Buckminster Fuller publishes *Operating Manual for Spaceship Earth*.

Irish novelist Elizabeth Bowen publishes *Eva Trout*.

Japanese avant-garde writer Kōbō Abe publishes the novel *Moyetsukita chizu/The Ruined Map* about a detective looking for a missing person and eventually becoming that person.

British novelist Brigid Brophy publishes *In Transit*.

British writer Peter Dickinson publishes the children's fantasy *The Weathermonger*.

Italian director Luchino Visconti makes the film *The Damned*, starring Dirk Bogarde.

English director John Schlesinger makes his first US film, *Midnight Cowboy*, starring John Voigt and Dustin Hoffman.

Jane Fonda stars in Sidney Pollack's film *They Shoot Horses, Don't They?*, set in the Depression.

French film director Eric Rohmer makes *Ma Nuit chez Maud/My Night at Maud's*.

Japanese director Masahiro Shinoda films Chikamatsu Monzaemon's classic play *Shinjū ten no Amijima/Double Suicide*.

US director Sam Peckinpah's film *The Wild Bunch* is a violent debunking of the Western.

Italian film director Sergio Leone's *Once Upon a Time in the West* is regarded as his masterpiece.

US film *Easy Rider*, directed by and starring Dennis Hopper, is a breakthrough for actor Jack Nicholson.

Paul Newman and Robert Redford star as *Butch Cassidy and the Sundance Kid*.

French film director Claude Chabrol makes *La Femme infidèle*.

British film director Ken Loach makes *Kes* in the vernacular of the north of England; the film is shown with subtitles in the USA.

English director Ken Russell films D H Lawrence's novel *Women in Love* with Glenda Jackson, Alan Bates, and Oliver Reed.

Belgian film director Agnes Varda makes *Lions Love* in English, starring US underground film actress Viva.

The National Health by English dramatist Peter Nichols has its premiere at the Old Vic Theatre, London.

British actor Nicol Williamson plays **Hamlet** at the Round House in London, directed by Tony Richardson with pop singer Marianne Faithfull as Ophelia.

Peggy Ashcroft stars in US dramatist Edward Albee's *A Delicate Balance* at the Aldwych Theatre, London.

English dramatist David Storey's *In Celebration* has its premiere at the Royal Court Theatre, London, directed by Lindsay Anderson.

Italian avant-garde composer Luciano Berio writes *Sinfonia* for voices and orchestra.

US soprano **Jessye Norman** gives her first operatic performance at the Deutsche Opera, Berlin.

English composer Peter Maxwell Davies writes *Vesalii Icones* for nude dancer, solo cellist, and ensemble.

English avant-garde composer Harrison Birtwhistle composes *Verses for Ensembles* for the London Sinfonietta.

Breakthrough year for US rock band **Creedence Clearwater Revival**; their hits, written by John Fogerty, include 'Proud Mary' and 'Bad Moon Rising'.

The Stooges is the first album of Iggy Pop and arguably the first punk LP; it is produced by John Cale, who has just left the Velvet Underground.

English folk-rock band Fairport Convention release the seminal albums *Unhalfbricking* and *Liege and Lief*.

Heavy metal is developed by English rock group Led Zeppelin, who release their first two (eponymous) albums (Feb and Oct).

The **Comme des Garçons** fashion house is started by Japanese designer Rei Kawakubo. Her avant-garde designs will be influential in the 1980s.

Soviet grandmaster **Boris Spassky** becomes world chess champion.

US baseball player **Mickey Mantle** retires after 18 years with the Yankees team.

American football player **Joe Namath** leads the Jets to victory in the Super Bowl.

Soviet ice skater **Irina Rodnina** becomes world champion in pairs competitions.

Scottish motor-racing driver **Jackie Stewart** becomes world champion for the first of three times, for Matra.

Liberation theology (Jesus' primary importance as the 'Liberator' freeing the poor from oppression) emerges as a left-wing movement in the Roman Catholic Church.

Nothing happened in the sixties except that we all dressed up.
John Lennon

Sixties' Facts

population of the world (millions)

1960	3,000	1965	3,300
1962	3,100	1969	3,500

world's largest countries

year	country	million inhabitants
1961	China	650
	India	445
	USSR	215
	USA	185
	Indonesia	100

world's largest cities

year	city	million inhabitants
1961	New York (metropolitan area)	14.2
	Tokyo	10.0
	London	8.3
	Paris	7.7
	Shanghai	7.1

social security as percentage of gross national product 1966

	GNP per head of population	social security
UK	$1,532	4.4%
Sweden	$2,677	17.5%
France	$1,866	8.3%
USSR	$1,181	11.2%
Poland	$762	9.4%

ITV advertising revenue

1960	£76,960,000	1965	£82,840,000
1961	£93,276,000	1966	£85,825,000
1962	£99,794,000	1967	£91,776,000
1963	£62,932,000	1968	£98,759,000
1964	£74,433,000	1969	£97,540,000

NB Figures from 1963 onwards are net of payments on commissions and discounts.

popular-music charts, UK singles

1960

week ending	title	artist
3 Jan	'What Do You Want?'	Adam Faith
10–24 Jan	'What Do You Want to Make Those Eyes at Me For?'	Emile Ford
31 Jan	'Starry Eyed'	Michael Holliday
7–28 Feb	'Why?'	Anthony Newley
6–13 March	'Poor Me'	Adam Faith
20 March	'Running Bear'	Johnny Preston
27 March–18 April	'My Old Man's a Dustman'	Lonnie Donegan
25 April	'Do You Mind?'	Anthony Newley
1 May–14 June	'Cathy's Clown'	the Everly Brothers
21 June–17 July	'Good Timin''	Jimmy Jones
24 July–14 Aug	'Please Don't Tease'	Cliff Richard
21 Aug–25 Sept	'Apache'	the Shadows
2 Oct	'Tell Laura I Love Her'	Ricky Valance
9-23 Oct	'Only the Lonely'	Roy Orbison
30 Oct–18 Dec	'It's Now or Never'	Elvis Presley
25 Dec	'Poetry in Motion'	Johnny Tillotson

1961

week ending	title	artist
1–22 Jan	'Poetry in Motion'	Johnny Tillotson
29 Jan–26 Feb	'Are You Lonesome Tonight?'	Elvis Presley
5–19 March	'Walk Right Back'	the Everly Brothers
26 March–2 April	'Wooden Heart'	Elvis Presley
9 April	'Are You Sure?'	the Allisons
16–23 April	'Wooden Heart'	Elvis Presley
30 April	'You're Driving Me Crazy'	the Temperance Seven
7–14 May	'Blue Moon'	the Marcels
21	'Runaway'	Del Shannon
28 May–18 June	'Surrender'	Elvis Presley
25 June–16 July	'Runaway'	Del Shannon
23–30 July	'Temptation'	the Everly Brothers
7 Aug	'Well I Ask You'	Eden Kane
14 Aug	'You Don't Know'	Helen Shapiro
21 Aug–8 Oct	'Johnny Remember Me'	John Leyton

15 Oct	'Michael'	the Highwaymen
22 Oct–12 Nov	'Walkin' Back to Happiness'	Helen Shapiro
19 Nov–3 Dec	'His Latest Flame'	Elvis Presley
10 Dec	'Take Good Care of My Baby'	Bobby Vee
17–31 Dec	'Tower of Strength'	Frankie Vaughan

1962

week ending	title	artist
6 –13 Jan	'Moon River'	Danny Williams
20 Jan–24 Feb	'The Young Ones'	Cliff Richard
3–10 March	'Let's Twist Again'	Chubby Checker
17–24 March	'March of the Siamese Children'	Kenny Ball
31 March–19 May	'Wonderful Land'	the Shadows
26 May–23 Jun	'Good Luck Charm'	Elvis Presley
30 June	'Come Outside'	Mike Sarne
7 July	'Good Luck Charm'	Elvis Presley
14–21 July	'I Can't Stop Loving You'	Ray Charles
28 July–15 Sept	'I Remember You'	Frank Ifield
22 Sept–6 Oct	'She's Not You'	Elvis Presley
13 Oct–10 Nov	'Telstar'	the Tornadoes
17 Nov–15 Dec	'Lovesick Blues'	Frank Ifield
22-29 Dec	'Return to Sender'	Elvis Presley

1963

week ending	title	artist
5–19Jan	'The Next Time/ Bachelor Boy'	Cliff Richard
26 Jan	'Dance On'	the Shadows
2–16 Feb	'Diamonds'	Jet Harris and Tony Meehan
23 Feb–9 March	'Wayward Wind'	Frank Ifield
16–23 March	'Summer Holiday'	Cliff Richard
30 March	'Foot Tapper'	the Shadows
6–20 April	'How Do You Do It?'	Gerry and the Pacemakers
27 April–25 May	'From Me to You'	the Beatles
1–8 June	'Do You Want to Know a Secret'	Billy J Kramer and the Dakotas

15 June–6 July	'I Like It'	Gerry and the Pacemakers
13–27 July	'I'm Confessin''	Frank Ifield
3–17 Aug	'Sweets for My Sweet'	the Searchers
24–31 Aug	'Bad to Me'	Billy J Kramer and the Dakotas
7–28 Sept	'She Loves You'	the Beatles
5–19 Oct	'Do You Love Me?'	Brian Poole and the Tremeloes
26 Oct–23 Nov	'You'll Never Walk Alone'	Gerry and the Pacemakers
30 Nov	'She Loves You'	the Beatles
7–28 Dec	'I Want to Hold Your Hand'	the Beatles

1964

week ending	title	artist
4–11 Jan	'I Want to Hold Your Hand'	the Beatles
18–25 Jan	'Glad All Over'	the Dave Clark Five
1–15 Feb	'Needles and Pins'	the Searchers
22 Feb–14 March	'Anyone Who Had a Heart'	Cilla Black
21 March	'Little Children'	Billy J Kramer and the Dakotas
28 March–18 April	'Can't Buy Me Love'	the Beatles
25 April–2 May	'World without Love'	Peter and Gordon
9–16 May	'Don't Throw Your Love Away'	the Searchers
23 May	'Juliet'	the Four Pennies
30 May–20 June	'You're My World'	Cilla Black
27 June–18 July	'It's Over'	Roy Orbison
25 July	'The House of the Rising Sun'	the Animals
1–22 Aug	'A Hard Day's Night'	the Beatles
29 Aug–5 Sept	'Do Wah Diddy Diddy'	Manfred Mann
12–19 Sept	'Have I the Right'	the Honeycombs
26 Sept	'You Really Got Me'	the Kinks
3 Oct	'I'm into Something Good'	Herman's Hermits
10–17 Oct	'Oh, Pretty Woman'	Roy Orbison

24 Oct–7 Nov	'Always Something There to Remind Me'	Sandie Shaw
14 Nov	'Oh, Pretty Woman'	Roy Orbison
21–28 Nov	'Baby Love'	the Supremes
5 Dec	'Little Red Rooster'	the Rolling Stones
12–26 Dec	'I Feel Fine'	the Beatles

1965

week ending	title	artist
2–23 Jan	'I Feel Fine'	the Beatles
30 Jan	'Yeh, Yeh'	Georgie Fame
7–14 Feb	'Go Now'	the Moody Blues
21 Feb	'You've Lost That Lovin' Feelin''	the Righteous Brothers
28 Feb	'Tired of Waiting for You'	the Kinks
7–14 March	'I'll Never Find Another You'	the Seekers
21 March	'It's Not Unusual'	Tom Jones
28 March	'The Last Time'	the Rolling Stones
4 April	'For Your Love'	the Yardbirds
11 April–9 May	'Ticket to Ride'	the Beatles
16 May	'Where Are You Now?'	Jackie Trent
23–30 May	'Long Live Love'	Sandie Shaw
6 June	'Price of Love'	the Everly Brothers
13–20 June	'Crying in the Chapel'	Elvis Presley
27 June–4 July	'I'm Alive'	the Hollies
11–18 July	'Mr Tambourine Man'	Bob Dylan
25 July–15 Aug	'Help!'	the Beatles
22 Aug	'I Got You Babe'	Sonny and Cher
29 Aug–12 Sept	'(I Can't Get No) Satisfaction'	the Rolling Stones
19 Sept–24 Oct	'Tears'	Ken Dodd
31 Oct–21 Nov	'Get Off My Cloud'	the Rolling Stones
28 Nov	'1–2–3'	Len Barry
5–26 Dec	'Day Tripper/We Can Work It Out'	the Beatles

1966

week ending	title	artist
1 Jan	'Day Tripper/We Can Work It Out'	the Beatles

8–22 Jan	'Keep On Running'	the Spencer Davis Group
29 Jan	'Michelle'	the Overlanders
5 Feb	'These Boots Are Made for Walkin''	Nancy Sinatra
12–19 Feb	'Keep On Running'	the Spencer Davis Group
26 Feb	'19th Nervous Breakdown'	the Rolling Stones
5 March	'I Can't Let Go'	the Hollies
12 March–9 April	'The Sun Ain't Gonna Shine Anymore'	the Walker Brothers
16 April	'Somebody Help Me'	the Spencer Davis Group
23–30 April	'You Don't Have to Say You Love Me'	Dusty Springfield
7–21 May	'Pretty Flamingo'	Manfred Mann
28 May	'Paint It Black'	the Rolling Stones
4–18 June	'Strangers in the Night'	Frank Sinatra
25 June–2 July	'Paperback Writer'	the Beatles
9–16 July	'Sunny Afternoon'	the Kinks
23–30 July	'Out of Time'	Chris Farlowe
6–13 Aug	'A Girl Like You'	the Troggs
20 Aug–10 Sept	'Yellow Submarine/ Eleanor Rigby'	the Beatles
17 Sept	'All Or Nothing'	the Small Faces
24 Sept–22 Oct	'Distant Drums'	Jim Reeves
29 Oct–5 Nov	'Reach Out I'll Be There'	the Four Tops
12 Nov	'Love Is a Hurtin' Thing'	Lou Rawls
19–26 Nov	'Good Vibrations'	the Beach Boys
3–31 Dec	'Green Green Grass of Home'	Tom Jones

1967

week ending	title	artist
7 Jan	'Green Green Grass of Home'	Tom Jones
14 Jan–4 Feb	'I'm a Believer'	the Monkees
11–18 Feb	'This Is My Song'	Petula Clark
25 Feb–2 April	'Release Me'	Engelbert Humperdinck
9 April	'Somethin' Stupid'	Frank and Nancy Sinatra
16 April–7 May	'Puppet on a String'	Sandie Shaw
14 May–5 June	'Silence Is Golden'	the Tremeloes
12 June–10 July	'A Whiter Shade of Pale'	Procol Harum

17 July–7 Aug	'All You Need Is Love'	the Beatles
14 Aug–2 Sept	'San Francisco (Be Sure to Wear Flowers in Your Hair)'	Scott McKenzie
9 Sept–14 Oct	'The Last Waltz'	Engelbert Humperdinck
21 Oct–4 Nov	'Massachusetts'	the Bee Gees
11–25 Nov	'Baby, Now That I've Found You'	the Foundations
2 Dec	'Let the Heartaches Begin'	Long John Baldry
9–30 Dec	'Hello Goodbye'	the Beatles

1968

week ending	title	artist
6–13 Jan	'Hello Goodbye'	the Beatles
20 Jan	'The Ballad of Bonnie and Clyde'	Georgie Fame
27 Jan–10 Feb	'Everlasting Love'	Love Affair
17–24 Feb	'Mighty Quinn'	Manfred Mann
2–16 March	'Cinderella Rockefella'	Esther and Abi Ofarim
30 March–6 April	'Lady Madonna'	the Beatles
13 April	'Congratulations'	Cliff Richard
20 April–11 May	'What a Wonderful World'	Louis Armstrong
18 May–15 June	'Young Girl'	Gary Puckett and the Union Gap
22 June	'Jumpin' Jack Flash'	the Rolling Stones
6–20 July	'Baby Come Back'	the Equals
27 July–17 Aug	'Mony Mony'	Tommy James and the Shondells
24–31 Aug	'Help Yourself'	Tom Jones
7 Sept	'I've Got to Get a Message to You'	the Bee Gees
14–28 Sept	'Hey Jude'	the Beatles
5 Oct–2 Nov	'Those Were the Days'	Mary Hopkin
9 Nov	'With a Little Help from My Friends'	Joe Cocker
16 Nov	'The Good, the Bad and the Ugly'	Hugo Montenegro
23–30 Nov	'Eloise'	Barry Ryan
7–28 Dec	'Lily the Pink'	the Scaffold

1969

week ending	title	artist
4 Jan	'Lily the Pink'	the Scaffold
11–18 Jan	'Ob-La-Di, Ob-La-Da'	the Beatles
25 Jan–8 Feb	'Albatross'	Fleetwood Mac
15 Feb	'Blackberry Way'	the Move
22 Feb	'Half as Nice'	Amen Corner
1–22 March	'Where Do You Go to (My Lovely)?'	Peter Sarstedt
29 March–5 April	'I Heard It Through the Grapevine'	Marvin Gaye
12–26 April	'The Israelites'	Desmond Dekker
3–31 May	'Get Back'	the Beatles
7–14 June	'Dizzy'	Tommy Roe
21–28 June	'The Ballad of John and Yoko'	the Beatles
5–12 July	'Something in the Air'	Thunderclap Newman
19 July	'In the Ghetto'	Elvis Presley
26 July–23 Aug	'Honky Tonk Women'	the Rolling Stones
30 Aug–13 Sept	'In the Year 2525'	Zager and Evans
20 Sept–4 Oct	'Bad Moon Rising'	Creedence Clearwater Revival
11–25 Oct	'I'll Never Fall in Love Again'	Bobbie Gentry
1–8 Nov	'Sugar, Sugar'	the Archies
15 Nov	'Oh Well'	Fleetwood Mac
22–29 Nov	'Sugar, Sugar'	the Archies
6 Dec	'Yester-Me, Yester-You, Yesterday'	Stevie Wonder
13 Dec	'Ruby, Don't Take Your Love to Town'	Kenny Rogers and the First Edition
20–27 Dec	'Two Little Boys'	Rolf Harris

popular-music charts, UK albums

1964

18 July–5 Dec	*A Hard Day's Night*	the Beatles
12–26 Dec	*Beatles for Sale*	the Beatles

1965

2–16 Jan	*Beatles for Sale*	the Beatles

23 Jan–11 April	*The Rolling Stones No. 2*	the Rolling Stones
18 April–2 May	*Beatles for Sale*	the Beatles
9 May	*The Freewheelin' Bob Dylan*	Bob Dylan
16 May–13 June	*Bringing It All Back Home*	Bob Dylan
20 June	*The Sound of Music*	soundtrack
27 June–11 July	*Bringing It All Back Home*	Bob Dylan
18 July–1 Aug	*The Sound of Music*	soundtrack
8 Aug–17 Oct	*Help*	the Beatles
24 Oct–28 Nov	*The Sound of Music*	soundtrack
5–26 Dec	*Rubber Soul*	the Beatles

1966

1 Jan–19 Feb	*Rubber Soul*	the Beatles
26 Feb–23 April	*The Sound of Music*	soundtrack
30 April–25 June	*Aftermath*	the Rolling Stones
2 July–6 Aug	*The Sound of Music*	soundtrack
13 Aug–24 Sept	*Revolver*	the Beatles
1 Oct–31 Dec	*The Sound of Music*	soundtrack

1967

7–28 Jan	*The Sound of Music*	soundtrack
4 Feb–18 March	*The Monkees*	the Monkees
25 March	*The Sound of Music*	soundtrack
2 April	*The Monkees*	the Monkees
9 April–28 May	*The Sound of Music*	soundtrack
5 June–14 Oct	*Sgt Pepper's Lonely Hearts Club Band*	the Beatles
21 Oct–30 Dec	*The Sound of Music*	soundtrack

1968

6-13 Jan	*Sgt Pepper's Lonely Hearts Club Band*	the Beatles
20 Jan	*Val Doonican Rocks, but Gently*	Val Doonican
27 Jan	*The Sound of Music*	soundtrack
3 Feb–9 March	*Greatest Hits*	the Supremes
16 March–27 April	*John Wesley Harding*	Bob Dylan
4 May–22 June	*This Is Soul*	various

6–27 July	*Ogden's Nut Gone Flake*	the Small Faces
3 Aug	*Bookends*	Simon and Garfunkel
10 Aug	*Delilah*	Tom Jones
17 Aug–7 Sept	*Bookends*	Simon and Garfunkel
14 Sept–23 Nov	*Greatest Hits*	the Hollies
30 Nov–14 Dec	*The Beatles*	the Beatles
28 Dec	*The Sound of Music*	soundtrack

1969

4–25 Jan	*The Beatles*	the Beatles
1 Feb	*The Best of the Seekers*	the Seekers
8 Feb–15 March	*Diana Ross and the Supremes join the Temptations*	the Supremes and the Temptations
22 March–3 May	*Goodbye*	Cream
10–17 May	*On the Threshold of a Dream*	the Moody Blues
24 May–14 June	*Nashville Skyline*	Bob Dylan
21–28 June	*My Way*	Frank Sinatra
5–26 July	*This Is Tom Jones*	Tom Jones
2 Aug	*Flaming Star*	Elvis Presley
9 Aug–13 Sept	*Stand Up*	Jethro Tull
20–27 Sept	*At San Quentin*	Johnny Cash
4 Oct–27 Dec	*Abbey Road*	the Beatles

Grammy awards

(given by the US National Academy of Recording Arts and Sciences)

year	*single of the year* *(album of the year)*	*artist* *artist*
1960	'Theme from *A Summer Place*' *Button-Down Mind*	Percy Faith Bob Newhart
1961	'Moon River' *Judy at Carnegie Hall*	Henry Mancini Judy Garland
1962	'I Left My Heart in San Francisco' *The First Family*	Tony Bennett Vaughn Meader
1963	'The Days of Wine and Roses' *The Barbra Streisand Album*	Henry Mancini Barbra Streisand

1964	'The Girl from Ipanema'	Stan Getz and Astrud Gilberto
	Getz/Gilberto	Stan Getz and Joao Gilberto
1965	'A Taste of Honey'	Herb Alpert and the Tijuana Brass
	September of My Years	Frank Sinatra
1966	'Strangers in the Night'	Frank Sinatra
	Sinatra: A Man and His Music	Frank Sinatra
1967	'Up, Up and Away'	5th Dimension
	Sgt Pepper's Lonely Heart's Club Band	the Beatles
1968	'Mrs Robinson'	Simon and Garfunkel
	By the Time I Get to Phoenix	Glen Campbell
1969	'Aquarius/Let the Sunshine In'	5th Dimension
	Blood, Sweat & Tears	Blood, Sweat & Tears

UK best-selling singles

1960	'Cathy's Clown'	the Everly Brothers
1961	'Runaway'	Del Shannon
1962	'Stranger On The Shore'	Acker Bilk
1963	'From Me To You'	the Beatles
1964	'I Love You Because'	Jim Reeves
1965	'I'll Never Find Another You'	the Seekers
1966	'Distant Drums'	Jim Reeves
1967	'Release Me'	Engelbert Humperdinck
1968	'What a Wonderful World'	Louis Armstrong
1969	'My Way'	Frank Sinatra

Pulitzer Prize for Fiction

1960	Allen Drury	*Advise and Consent*
1961	Harper Lee	*To Kill a Mockingbird*
1962	Edwin O'Connor	*The Edge of Sadness*
1963	William Faulkner	*The Reivers*
1964	no award	
1965	Shirley Ann Grau	*The Keepers of the House*
1966	Katherine Anne Porter	*The Collected Stories of Katherine Anne Porter*
1967	Bernard Malamud	*The Fixer*
1969	N Scott Momaday	*House Made of Dawn*

Nobel Prize for Literature

1960	Saint-John Perse (French)
1961	Ivo Andric (Yugoslav)
1962	John Steinbeck (American)
1963	George Seferis (Greek)
1964	Jean-Paul Sartre, declined award (French)
1965	Mikhail Sholokhov (Russian)
1966	Shmuel Yosef Agnon (Israeli)
	Nelly Sachs (German-born Swedish)
1967	Miguel Angel Asturias (Guatemalan)
1969	Samuel Beckett (Irish)

Motion picture Academy Awards (Oscars)

1960 Best Picture: *The Apartment*; Best Director: Billy Wilder *The Apartment*; Best Actor: Burt Lancaster *Elmer Gantry*; Best Actress: Elizabeth Taylor *Butterfield 8*

1961 Best Picture: *West Side Story*; Best Director: Robert Wise and Jerome Robbins *West Side Story*; Best Actor: Maximillian Schell *Judgment at Nuremberg*; Best Actress: Sophia Loren *Two Women*

1962 Best Picture: *Lawrence of Arabia*; Best Director: David Lean *Lawrence of Arabia*; Best Actor: Gregory Peck *To Kill A Mockingbird*; Best Actress: Anne Bancroft *The Miracle Worker*

1963 Best Picture: *Tom Jones*; Best Director: Tony Richardson *Tom Jones*; Best Actor: Sidney Poitier *Lilies of the Field*; Best Actress: Patricia Neal *Hud*

1964 Best Picture: *My Fair Lady*; Best Director: George Cukor *My Fair Lady*; Best Actor: Rex Harrison *My Fair Lady*; Best Actress: Julie Andrews *My Fair Lady*

1965 Best Picture: *The Sound of Music*; Best Director: Robert Wise *The Sound of Music*; Best Actor: Lee Marvin *Cat Ballou*; Best Actress:Julie Christie *Darling*

1966 Best Picture: *A Man for All Seasons*; Best Director: Fred Zinnemann *A Man for All Seasons*; Best Actor: Paul Scofield *A Man for All Seasons*; Best Actress: Elizabeth Taylor *Who's Afraid of Virginia Woolf?*

1967 Best Picture: *In the Heat of the Night*; Best Director: Mike Nichols *The Graduate*; Best Actor: Rod Steiger *In the Heat of the Night*; Best Actress: Katherine Hepburn *Guess Who's Coming to Dinner?*

1968	Best Picture: *Oliver!*; Best Director: Sir Carol Reed *Oliver!*; Best Actor: Cliff Robertson *Charly*; Best Actress: Katherine Hepburn *The Lion in Winter* and Barbra Streisand *Funny Girl*
1969	Best Picture: *Midnight Cowboy*; Best Director: John Schlesinger *Midnight Cowboy*; Best Actor: John Wayne *True Grit*; Best Actress: Maggie Smith *The Prime of Miss Jean Brodie*

Association Football

World Cup winners		*European Championship winners*	
1962	Brazil	1960	USSR
1966	England	1964	Spain
		1968	Italy

Boxing World Champions

Heavyweight

1960	Floyd Patterson (USA)
1962	Sonny Liston (USA)
1964	Cassius Clay (USA)
1965	Ernie Terrell (USA) WBA
1968	Jimmy Ellis (USA) WBA

Light Heavyweight

1962	Harold Johnson (USA)
1963	Willie Pastrano (USA)
1965	Jose Torres (PR)
1966	Dick Tiger (NIG)
1968	Bob Foster (USA)

Middleweight

1960	Paul Pender (USA)
1961	Terry Downes (GB)
1962	Paul Pender (USA)
1962	Dick Tiger (NIG)
1963	Joey Giardello (USA)
1965	Dick Tiger (NIG)
1966	Emile Griffith (VI)
1968	Nino Benvenuti (ITA)

Welterweight

1960	Benny Kid Paret (CUB)
1961	Emile Griffith (VIR)
1961	Benny Kid Paret (CUB)
1962	Emile Griffith (VIR)
1963	Luis Rodriguez (CUB)
1963	Emile Griffith (VIR)
1966	Curtis Cokes (USA)
1969	Jose Napoles (CUB)

Lightweight

1962	Carlos Ortiz (PR)
1965	Ismael Laguna (PAN)
1965	Carlos Ortiz (PR)
1968	Carlos Teo Cruz (DOM)
1969	Mando Ramos (USA)

Featherweight

1963	Sugar Ramos (CUB)
1964	Vicente Saldivar (MEX)
1968	Howard Winstone (GB) WBC
1968	Raul Rojas (USA) WBA
1968	Jose Legra (CUB) WBC
1968	Shozo Saijyo (JAP) WBA
1969	Johnny Famechon (FRA) WBC

Bantamweight

1960	Eder Jofre (BRA)
1965	Fighting Harada (JAP)
1968	Lionel Rose (AUS)
1969	Ruben Olivares (MEX)

Flyweight

1960	Pone Kingpetch (THA)
1962	Fighting Harada (JAP)
1963	Pone Kingpetch (THA)
1963	Hiroyuki Ebihara (JAP)
1964	Pone Kingpetch (THA)
1965	Salvatore Burruni (ITA)
1966	Horacio Accavallo (ARG) WBA
1966	Walter McGowan (GB) WBC
1966	Chartchai Chionoi (THAI) WBC

1969	Efren Torres (MEX) WBC
1969	Hiroyuki Ebihara (JAP) WBA
1969	Bernabe Villacampo (PHI) WBA

Cricket

County Champions

1960	Yorkshire	1965	Worcestershire
1961	Hampshire	1966	Yorkshire
1962	Yorkshire	1967	Yorkshire
1963	Yorkshire	1968	Yorkshire
1964	Worcestershire	1969	Glamorgan

Golf

British Open Championship Winners

1960	K Nagle (AUS)	1965	P Thomson (AUS)
1961	A D Palmer (USA)	1966	J W Nicklaus (USA)
1962	A D Palmer (USA)	1967	R de Vicenzo (ARG)
1963	R Charles (NZ)	1968	G Player (SAF)
1964	A Lema (USA)	1969	A Jacklin (GB)

Ryder Cup Winners

1961	United States	1967	United States
1963	United States	1969	drawn
1965	United States		

United States Open Championship Winners

1960	A D Palmer	1965	G Player (SAF)
1961	G Littler	1966	W Casper
1962	J W Nicklaus	1967	J W Nicklaus
1963	J Boros	1968	L Trevino
1964	K Venturi	1969	O Moody

Lawn Tennis

Wimbledon champions

Men's singles		Women's singles	
1960	N A Fraser (AUS)	1960	M E Bueno (BRA)
1961	R G Laver (AUS)	1961	A Mortimer (GB)
1962	R G Laver (AUS)	1962	J R Susman (USA)
1963	C R McKinley (USA)	1963	M Smith (AUS)
1964	R S Emerson (AUS)	1964	M E Bueno (BRA)

Men's singles cont.		*Women's singles cont.*	
1965	R S Emerson (AUS)	**1965**	M Smith (AUS)
1966	M Santana (SPA)	**1966**	L W King (USA)
1967	J D Newcombe (AUS)	**1967**	L W King (USA)
1968	R G Laver (AUS)	**1968**	L W King (USA)
1969	R G Laver (AUS)	**1969**	P F Jones (GB)

Men's doubles

1960	R H Osuna (MEX) R D Ralston (USA)
1961	R Emerson(AUS) N A Fraser (AUS)
1962	R A J Hewitt (AUS) F S Stolle (AUS)
1963	R H Osuna (MEX) A Palafox (MEX)
1964	R A J Hewitt (AUS) F S Stolle (AUS)
1965	J D Newcombe (AUS) A D Roche (AUS)
1966	K N Fletcher (AUS J D Newcombe (AUS)
1967	R A J Hewitt (SAF) F D McMillan (SAF)
1968	J D Newcombe (AUS) A D Roche (AUS)
1969	J D Newcombe (AUS) A D Roche (AUS)

Women's doubles

1960	M E Bueno (BRA) D R Hard (USA)
1961	K Hantz (USA) B J Moffitt (USA)
1962	B J Moffitt (USA) J R Susman (USA)
1963	M E Bueno (BRA) D R Hard (USA)
1964	M Smith (AUS) L R Turner (AUS)
1965	M E Bueno (BRA) B J Moffitt (USA)
1966	M E Bueno (BRA) N Richey (USA)
1967	R Casals (USA) L W King (USA)
1968	R Casals (USA) L W King (USA)
1969	B M Court (AUS) J A M Tegart (AUS)

Mixed doubles

1960	R G Laver (AUS) D R Hard (USA)
1961	F S Stolle (AUS) L R Turner (AUS)
1962	N A Fraser (AUS) M Osborne-Du Pont (USA)
1963	K N Fletcher (AUS) M Smith (AUS)
1964	F S Stolle (AUS) L R Turner (AUS)
1965	K N Fletcher (AUS) M Smith (AUS)
1966	K N Fletcher (AUS) M Smith (AUS)
1967	O K Davidson (AUS) L W King (USA)
1968	K N Fletcher (AUS)B M Court (AUS)
1969	F S Stolle (AUS) P F Jones (GB)

Rugby League

Challenge Cup winners

1960	Wakefield Town	1965	Wigan
1961	St Helens	1966	St Helens
1962	Wakefield Town	1967	Featherstone Rovers
1963	Wakefield Town	1968	Leeds
1964	Widnes	1969	Castleford

World Cup winners

1960	Great Britain	1968	Australia

Rugby Union

International Championship winners

1960	France, England	1965	Wales
1961	France	1966	Wales
1962	France	1967	France
1963	England	1968	France
1964	Scotland, Wales	1969	Wales

County Championship winners

1960	Warwickshire	1965	Warwickshire
1961	Cheshire	1966	Middlesex
1962	Warwickshire	1967	Surrey and Durham
1963	Warwickshire	1968	Middlesex
1964	Warwickshire	1969	Lancashire

Nobel Prize for Physics

1960	Donald Glaser (USA): invention of the bubble chamber
1961	Robert Hofstadter (USA): scattering of electrons in atomic nuclei, and structure of protons and neutrons. Rudolf Mössbauer (Germany): resonance absorption of gamma radiation
1962	Lev Landau (USSR): theories of condensed matter, especially liquid helium
1963	Eugene Wigner (USA): discovery and application of symmetry principles in atomic physics. Maria Goeppert-Mayer (USA): and Hans Jensen (Germany): discovery of the shell-like structure of atomic nuclei
1964	Charles Townes (USA), Nikolai Basov (USSR), and Aleksandr Prokhorov (USSR): quantum electronics leading

	to construction of oscillators and amplifiers based on maser–laser principle
1965	Sin-Itiro Tomonaga (Japan), Julian Schwinger (USA), and Richard Feynman (USA): quantum electrodynamics
1966	Alfred Kastler (France): development of optical pumping, whereby atoms are raised to higher energy levels by illumination
1967	Hans Bethe (USA) theory of nuclear reactions, and discoveries concerning production of energy in stars
1968	Luis Alvarez (USA): elementary-particle physics, and discovery of resonance states, using hydrogen bubble chamber and data analysis
1969	Murray Gell-Mann (USA): classification of elementary particles, and study of their interactions

Nobel Prize for Physiology or Medicine

1960	Macfarlane Burnet (Australia) and Peter Medawar (UK): acquired immunological tolerance of transplanted tissues
1961	Georg von Békésy (USA): investigations into the mechanisms of hearing within the cochlea of the inner ear
1962	Francis Crick (UK), James Watson (USA), and Maurice Wilkins (UK): discovery of the double-helical structure of DNA and the significance of this structure in the replication and transfer of genetic information
1963	John Eccles (Australia), Alan Hodgkin (UK), and Andrew Huxley (UK): ionic mechanisms involved in the communication or inhibition of impulses across neuron (nerve cell) membranes
1964	Konrad Bloch (USA) and Feodor Lynen (West Germany): cholesterol and fatty acid metabolism
1965	François Jacob (France), André Lwoff (France), and Jacques Monod (France): genetic control of enzyme and virus synthesis
1966	Peyton Rous (USA): discovery of tumour-inducing viruses; Charles Huggins (USA): hormonal treatment of prostatic cancer
1967	Ragnar Granit (Sweden), Haldan Hartline (USA), and George Wald (USA): physiology and chemistry of vision
1968	Robert Holley (USA), Har Gobind Khorana (USA), and Marsall Nirenberg (USA): interpretation of genetic code and its function in protein synthesis

| 1969 | Max Delbruck (USA), Alfred Hershey (USA), and Salvador Luria (USA): replication mechanism and genetic structure of viruses |

Civil wars and related battles

1960–67	Congolese Civil War	Secession attempt by Katanga from the Republic of the Congo (now Zaire).
1961–75	Angolan War of Independence	Three nationalist movements against Portuguese colonial rulers.
1961–	Kurdish revolts	Separatist uprisings by Kurds especially in Iraq and Iran.
1962–70	North Yemen Civil War	Royalists against republicans
1962–	Irian Jaya conflict	Popular resistance in W New Guinea to Indonesian rule.
1963–68	Cypriot Civil War	Turkish community in Cyprus withdrew recognition of Greek Cypriot government.
1963–	Eritrean revolt	Secessionist movement in N Ethiopia.
1964–74	Mozambique War of Independence	Nationalist opposition to Portuguese colonial rule.
1965–79	Zimbabwe Civil War	Popular resistance to white-only rule in what was then Rhodesia.
1965–	Chad Civil War	Resistance by Muslim north to government.
1966–89	Namibian War of Independence	Popular resistance to South African rule.
1967–70	Nigerian (Biafran) Civil War	Attempted secession of state of Biafra.
1969–	Northern Ireland Troubles	Civil insurgence against British rule in Northern Ireland.

Some facts and figures of the decade

1960

In the UK, the richest 10% of the people own 83% of the country's wealth.

In the tax year 1959-60, London and the southeast of England contain just under a quarter of the UK's taxable population but 39% of all incomes of £5,000 a year and over.

In the UK, 593,000 people are employed in the coal-mining industry.

London is still the only part of the UK where books on foreign cookery sell in any significant number.

Guatemala has 86,000 sq km/33,200 sq mi of tropical rainforest.

More than 300 million paperback books are sold this year in the USA.

1961

The unemployment rate in the USA is 6.7%.

The world's most populous countries are China, with (est) 650 million inhabitants; India, with 445 million; the USSR, 215 million; the USA, 185 million; and Indonesia, 100 million.

UK government expenditure as a percentage of gross domestic product is 35% and rising.

A census is held in the UK. The population has risen to 52,675,000.

In England and Wales, there are two divorces for every 1,000 married people.

People living on their own make up 12% of all UK households.

In inner London, 31% of households have no bath and a further 19% have to share a bathroom with other households; 37% lack hot running water. Only 45% of households have exclusive use of all the basic domestic amenities.

16% of the population of inner London was born outside the UK (up from 10% 1951); in Kensington, Paddington, Hampstead, and Westminster the figure is around 33%.

There is an 11% surplus of women over men in the 20–24 age group in London.

The US gross national product, the world's largest, reaches $521 billion.

1962

113 bn cigarettes are sold this year in the UK.

Lung cancer kills 41,000 people in the USA alone this year (up from 3,000 in 1930).

Television sets are now found in 90% of US households.

1963

Public expenditure as a proportion of gross national product is 34.3% in the UK, 34.5% in West Germany, and 29.2% in the USA; the trend is upwards.

In the USA, 19.5% of the population lives below the official poverty line.

In England and Wales, 44% of households own their homes; in inner London, however, only 16% do so.

In the UK, 5,000 sq km/1,900 sq mi of land, mainly farmland, has been paved over for roads or urban development since 1933.

The amount of smoke polluting London's air has diminished by 60% since 1953, but sulphur emissions have risen by 32% because of increased traffic.

The USA has 6% of the world's population and 66% of its cars.

1964

The standard rate of income tax in the UK is 39% (before the election).

Over 40% of the UK population own their homes.

About 60% of Britons take a holiday away from home, though most of them within the UK.

Britain's military spending (under the Conservatives) is about £2 billion a year, of which £350 million is spent overseas.

An LP record costs £1 12s 3d, equivalent to £16.31 in 1993 value.

More than 12 million British households have television licences.

1965

Only 2% of Britons are convinced atheists, 14% agnostics, and 94% are affiliated to some organized religion; about 10% are weekly church-goers.

Some 40% of the people who work in London would like to move to another part of the country.

The tobacco industry spends over $200 million on television advertising.

The population of the world is 3.3 billion.

1966

The immigrant population of Greater London and the West Midlands, with the UK's highest concentrations, is 3.2%; only the London boroughs of Brent and Hackney have over 7%.

Industrial production in the UK has risen by 57% since 1961; in West Germany it has risen by 185%.

People living alone form 15% of all households in the UK; the figure is rising.

There are three divorces for every 1,000 married people in England and Wales; the figure is rising rapidly.

The USA has 389,000 troops in South Vietnam by the end of the year.

1967

Britain has 2,116 industrial disputes and more than 2.7 million working days lost to strikes during the year.

126 trade unions in the UK have fewer than 100 members each.

1968

There are 550,000 US troops in Vietnam (Nov).

The cost of the Vietnam War is now running at $33 billion a year.

As Cubans adjust to Fidel Castro's economic system, voluntary labour accounts for 8–10% of all labour, but absenteeism from paid work is running at about 20%.

Nearly 40% of Indian children suffer learning impairment from malnutrition, according to the minister for food.

The USA produces almost 11 million motor vehicles; Japan 4 million; West Germany 3 million; the UK and France about 2.1 million each.

In the USA, 12.8% of the population lives under the official poverty line.

1969

Unemployment in the USA has fallen to 3.5%.

The UK has 3,116 industrial disputes this year, with more than 6.8 million working days lost to strikes.

There are 91,000 police officers in England and Wales.

In England and Wales, 4,180 km/2,600 mi of hedgerows has been destroyed each year since 1947.

Index